WORKABLE DESIGN

KENNIKAT PRESS

NATIONAL UNIVERSITY PUBLICATIONS

SERIES ON LITERARY CRITICISM

General Editor
EUGENE GOODHEART
Professor of Literature, Massachusetts Institute of Technology

John P. O'Neill

WORKABLE DESIGN

Action and Situation in the Fiction of Henry James

National University Publications
KENNIKAT PRESS • 1973
Port Washington, N.Y. • London

813. 4
On 2w
88753
May 1974

Library of Congress Catalog Card No.: 72-91176
ISBN: 0-8046-9031-6
Manufactured in the United States of America

Published by
Kennikat Press, Inc.
Port Washington, N.Y./London

For M. C. O.

ACKNOWLEDGMENTS

I wish to thank my wife Connie, who read and criticized parts of the manuscript, and who helped me in many other ways, at the most important times; Thomas C. Moser, for his advice, criticism, and generous encouragement; Richard Robillard, Philip Stratford, and Hugh Hood, of l'Université de Montréal, for their suggestions and for a great deal of listening. My thanks go also to the Canada Council for the grant which enabled me to complete my research.

CONTENTS

WORKABLE DESIGN

1

INTRODUCTION:
THE JAMESIAN DESIGN

This study began with the hope that a formal analysis of action and situation in the novels of Henry James might afford new insights and bypass several old arguments about his work.

Critics of James have usually stressed his skill as a psychologist.[1] They begin where James invites us to begin, with his characters, and construct analyses in the hope that their description of patterns of motive and choice will explain the work. It would seem at first only prudent to heed James's own maxim that character and action are inseparable in a successful work of fiction:

> When one says picture one says of a character, when one says novel one says of incident, and the terms may be transposed at will. What is character but the determination of incident? What is incident but the illustration of character? What is either a picture or a novel that is *not* of character?[2]

Indeed, we usually take it for granted that James's incidents illustrate his characters, or at least that they are intended to, and that his

---

1. For a discussion of this major tendency in Jamesian criticism in the light of my own reading of the novels, see the Appendix.
2. James, *Selected Literary Criticism*, p. 58.

3

characters "determine" incidents. These incidents are neither varied nor violent. By far the most common is a conversation between two people, their speech interspersed with even more subdued incidents, typically of the kind which James mentions in the passage immediately following the one I have quoted above:

> It is an incident for a woman to stand up with her hand resting on a table and look out at you in a certain way; or if it be not an incident I think it will be hard to say what it is.[3]

Although apparently chosen as a random example, this woman seems very familiar to readers of James. She could be Isabel Archer or Madame Merle, Kate Croy or Maggie Verver. Taking her for the moment in this representative way, we might pause and consider our reaction to her and to the action she initiates. The incident is made to seem striking, memorable, somehow important out of all proportion to its significance when considered outside of James's context. Like so many of his own incidents it is objectively commonplace, but it strikes the reasonably sympathetic reader with undeniable force. The question is why?

The answer offered by most critics of James would go somewhat as follows: the incident is a powerful and significant one because it dramatizes and objectifies the emotional process (of suspicion, anxiety, or, most probably, growing awareness) which the heroine is presently undergoing. The critic is likely to believe and to at least imply that the only way to explain the powerful effect of such a banal incident is to treat it as an illustration of character.[4] James's novel is made up of hundreds of such incidents, banal and at the same time curiously exciting. Surely, we say, following James's lead, the excitement flows from the vitality of the young woman herself, Isabel, Milly Theale, or one of the others, characters of sufficient autonomy to invest even the smallest gesture with the vitality of their personality. Thus, the study of character and of the technical means of depicting psychology and moral choice become the staples of Jamesian criticism.

To stay for the moment with our woman, standing with hand upon the table and looking at us "in a certain way": by explaining our response to this incident solely by reference to her character we pay

---

3. *Ibid.*, pp. 58-59.

4. As, for example, in this sentence from an article by Stallman: "In the final scene of *The Ambassadors,* in the last pose we get of Strether, he's leaning back in his chair, but with his eyes on 'a small ripe round melon' — not leaning forward now, but passively reflecting on life in all its minute particulars, taking things as they come, his curiosity mixed with indifference." Stallman, "The Sacred Rage," p. 47.

her a kind of compliment. To put it simply, we say that nothing happens except what she determines. But we also impose upon her a rigorous responsibility. For if we can analyse her gesture in this scene only, or even primarily, as an illustration of her character, then more important incidents, the rejection of a lover, for example, or her efforts to reconcile a mother and her son, must similarly be explained as dramatized expressions of moral or psychological tendencies in her character. If what happens in the novel is to be thought of always as an illustration of her character, then we may hold the young woman pretty strictly accountable for everything that happens.

James gave his heroines freedom, we insist, freedom from severe financial obligations, and, in this instance, freedom from the random but often coercive stream of incident and detail which in reality impedes and deflects the individual. In our interpretation of the scene at hand, we extend to the woman the freedom to make a *wholly expressive gesture*. In return, and in proportion to our sense of her freedom and power, we demand that the incident yield a good measure of meaning and that this meaning be consistent with previous judgments formed about her. Logic and consistency are the payment exacted by the critic from the character whose actions are judged to be wholly expressive.

If his characters are indeed free to make their gestures, the incidents in which they are involved, wholly expressive of themselves, then it is reasonable to continue our study of the Jamesian character and James's techniques of characterization. We had better do so, however, with the explicit acknowledgment that our analyses of incident of the novels lead us to startlingly different, often contradictory assessments of the characters they are meant to express.[5]

There are at least three possible explanations for this. The first admits that a careful study of even James's major characters reveals serious psychological and moral inconsistencies. The source of such inconsistency, according to such critics as Wayne Booth and Yvor Winters, is to be found in James's artistic or moral confusion.[6]

A second response to contradiction and critical controversy is to greet it as the inevitable result of the study of a complex and profound artist. This is the reply of the committed Jamesian, or rather—the dis-

---

5. To confine ourselves to the type of interpretation that discovers serious flaws in characters admired by earlier critics, we could cite the following: Quinn, "Morals and Motives," pp. 563-77; Firebaugh, "The Ververs," pp. 419-35; Wasiolek, "Maisie," pp. 167-72. The list could easily be extended.
6. W. Booth, *The Rhetoric of Fiction,* pp. 364-74; Winters, *In Defense of Reason,* pp. 300-43.

tinction is important—the Jamesian committed to the analytical reconstruction of James's characters as wholly plausible psychological and moral entities. In such analyses the critic has begun with the conviction that the creation of such entities is James's chief interest. Once such a conviction has been formed, it provides the context, implicit or explicit, for the critic's own reconstruction of the novel. That context is of course radically different from the one in which James's character actually appeared: analysis, after all, establishes a context of its own, for it cannot hope to duplicate the original context of the work. But whereas the critic's context is different, it cannot afford to mislead us when we return to the book. The notion of autonomous, consistently developed, morally and psychologically profound characters is immensely congenial to the critic, so congenial in fact that one may regard the Jamesian character, so conceived, as one of the vested interests of current literary scholarship. And continued controversy about the basic facts of interpretation may indicate that the meaning, resident within this or that character, is inexhaustible. But we might also entertain the suspicion, a third possible explanation for continual controversy over basic facts in James's novels, that the critic's context, his formulation of the very terms of his analysis, is misleading.

How can this suspicion be profitably entertained? And particularly, how entertain it in the face of evidence which suggests that James himself thought of the depiction of character as his chief aim? The present study treats five novels, chosen to represent James's major periods and the chief types of fiction he attempted.[7] It argues that further controversy over the classic questions of motivation in James is likely to prove futile; that one's answer to some of the subtlest questions about motivation must finally be an ingenuous and unashamed, "It isn't clear, and it isn't clear precisely because James wasn't interested in the degree and kind of clarity we now demand of him." Further, I argue that a way out of this dilemma can be found by taking a careful look at a long neglected element in James's work: the extraordinarily powerful rhetorical effects of the action and situations in which his characters appear.[8] Thirdly, although I cannot dis-

---

7. I have chosen to use the New York Edition throughout, partly in order to demonstrate that James's fascination for a certain type of action did not diminish during his period of major revision.

8. By action I mean a series of external or internal events, the selection and arrangement of which are managed by James so as to affect his reader's understanding of, and response toward a character. Also, action is the instrument for some substantial change in the character. It is thus distinguished from situation, as I employ the term, for situation is the arrangement of relationships or of facts

count the evidence from the Prefaces indicating James's professed bias toward characterization, I can try to demonstrate that the Notebooks offer us a different and more accurate account of his process of composition. Finally, I'll try to show that a strict attention to action and situation, as rhetorical instruments, is essential for a study of James, since these were precisely the means by which he attempted to make his central figure the locus of values so intensely meaningful to James as to slip the bonds of either morality or psychology.

To expect James to be as consistent and as profound as his friendliest critics have judged him to be is to do him a disservice. James, as a writer, was deeply moved by certain kinds of experience. He saw the chance to evoke a similar response in his readers and to this end he created characters and manipulated them within an action or situation. Just as even a casual reading of James reveals the central irony in the lives of his heroes—they are rich, or intelligent, or beautiful, but caught nevertheless—so also a close reading of the text will reveal that James's characters, as artistic creations, are neither so autonomous nor so lastingly plausible as we had taken them to be. The *character* of Isabel Archer, James's artistic construct, is finally no more splendidly autonomous than the woman who presides over Osmond's salon. Isabel, character and young woman, is in the novel to awaken us to the pathos of the loss of freedom. To this end James exploits her, the action, the narrator's tone, the other characters, even Madame Merle's richly sinister plot of betrayal, a motif which appears regularly enough in James's novels to make us doubt that incident is "but the illustration of character." (The illustration of Dorothea Brooke's character requires no such contrivance. Nor are George Eliot's heroines, taken by themselves, less plausible or consistently developed than James's. In fact they are more so. The difference is that James, working with a more limited scope and striving for a more resonantly pathetic effect, uses Madame Merle's plot to save Isabel from looking as silly as Dorothea occasionally does as she blithely sacrifices her freedom to Casaubon.)

Incident may illustrate character; it may also, and sometimes more importantly, orchestrate the reactions of the reader. When an

---

rather than of events. Rhetoric I take to be the strategy by which the gifted writer awakens and sustains interest in his character. In my argument I emphasize the emotional quality of this interest, and this is partly because I believe that critics have exaggerated the interest and the importance of James's moral ideas. Thus, I am chiefly concerned with the manner in which the Jamesian action and situation elicit, control, or fail to control, the sympathetic interest of the reader.

incident seems inconsistent with what we have taken to be the "given" of the character, we ought to ask ourselves whether, at this particular moment, James might be willing to take a chance on affronting consistency for the sake of achieving quite another effect. (Although I will go much deeper into the point later, it's worth saying at once that serious contradictions in the characters are likely to appear only after the third or fourth reading of one of James's novels. Once tolerably committed to him, we have to struggle hard to evade the effect he intends.)

It is not enough merely to summarize or add to the controversies surrounding the motivation of James's characters. What is necessary is to demonstrate that the desire to affect his reader in various, often extremely subtle ways may be observed in some other element of his work. One such element is the Jamesian action or situation, the striking features of which may best be seen by comparing it with plots which seem more appropriate to moral and psychological portraiture.

Consider several actions, plots in skeletal form. A young woman with enormous confidence in herself and her freedom unwittingly acts to enslave herself. A child tries to preserve herself and a certain integrity in a corrupt environment. A middle-aged man changes his moral attitudes. A youth struggles to resolve the tensions created in his life by the opposition of political belief and aesthetic sensibility. Each of these situations we might expect to interest the psychological novelist. For him their interest would lie in the already sharpened focus upon internal action, the process that each implies, perhaps also the very sparseness of the formulas, which offer almost limitless opportunity for specific psychological notation. Analysis might proceed unhampered by violent action or rigid conventions. The subjects seem admirably suited to the treatment of character.

Do they appear any less amenable to treatment when, by a rather more detailed description of the action, we outline what James has made of them? Isabel Archer's desire for personal liberty, by its very fervency, seems to drive her toward a personal submission as humiliating as her former ambitions were intense. She wants to be free and becomes, as James puts it, "ground in the mill of the conventional." Maisie Farange, at first utterly ignorant of sex, struggles to defend herself among adults whose promiscuity eventually becomes so extravagant as to constitute a kind of self-parody. Lambert Strether ends his journey by endorsing the liaison he has been trained from his youth to abhor and sent in middle age to destroy. "Poor" Hyacinth Robinson, whose dilemma is only feebly described by the term "conflict," seems caught in a polar opposition between anarchism and aestheticism, alternate desires to destroy and embrace all of European civilization.

We have only slightly expanded our description of situations apparently well suited to the preoccupations of the psychological novelist. One observes a certain pattern emerging out of and common to their actions: the process of the action moves character from one situation or condition through successive stages to a final resting point that is discovered to be in virtual polar opposition to the point of origin. A desire for freedom, or "life," or "consciousness," seemingly by the very energy with which James invests it, leads its possessor to submission or death or the numbed defeat of the intelligence. An instinct, an attitude, a spiritual quality struggles against a principle which does not merely oppose but seeks to negate it entirely. The terms of conflict are stark and irreconcilable. Reversals tend to be complete. Contradictory tendencies in a given character are sometimes, as in the case of Hyacinth Robinson, made to seem absolute in their mutual opposition, and the inevitable result is a terminal paralysis. The pattern which emerges from the Jamesian action is, for all of the subtle working of his art *within* its confines, rigid and stylized. It calls attention to itself as *design,* apart from what it contributes to characterization or moral drama. This design, which we might call the characteristic profile of the Jamesian action, is, I believe, even more distinctive a signature of the author than the Jamesian character "types" who have been so frequently described. It appears in most of James's novels and in almost all of his shorter pieces of fiction.

Observing the stylized pattern we have described, our psychological novelist might well begin to suffer doubts. Such a frame would indeed lend coherence to his dramatic portrait, but probably at the cost of a degree of autonomy he would wish to accord to his characters. Such a pattern might suggest to him a new way in which his character's freedom of development—cumulative, consistent, *natural* development—might well be compromised. For a character is simply not "free," however removed he may be from conventional deterrents, if in the mind of his creator he figures as one part of an action which, in its neatness and superbly balanced opposition, rivals the terms of a mathematical equation. A character so placed does not suggest an author's complete or even primary interest in psychological or moral notation, but rather his fascination with the evocative power (for surprise, suspense, dramatic revelation, irony) of the design itself. And such indeed was James's interest.

James's fascination with the rhetorical power of his design of polar conflict can be seen in the earliest stories. Here the action is often overtly violent, and death, betrayal, and supernatural forces intervene to heighten what might otherwise be taken as realistic portraiture. For example, in "The Story of a Year,"[9] published in 1865, James concentrates for most of the narrative on the psychological process by which a young girl allows her affection to wander from absent fiancé to new lover. The fiancé, a soldier in the Union Army, is wounded in battle, and the girl is stricken with grief, particularly since the young man's mother, the girl's rival for his affection, seizes for herself the role of nurse to the fallen hero. Up to this point the story appears to be the vehicle for portraiture, that of a young girl whose feelings are vague and transitory, except for her need to be loved. But James concludes the tale so as to make the psychology of the girl, or for that matter, of any of the characters, the least striking element of the tale.

The sequence of the action at the end is as follows: the young soldier unexpectedly revives under his mother's care and returns with her to the village where the heroine has allowed herself to drift into another engagement, with a local businessman. The mother, learning of this second engagement, promptly tells her son, who just as promptly dies, pausing only long enough to assure his fiancée that she will be happy in her marriage to his rival.

One is left with two impressions, equally damaging to the effect of the story. First, the young man's death imposes upon the girl the responsibility of a guilt both out of proportion to her crime and absurdly beyond her capacity to bear or understand. She's a butterfly whom the author chooses to destroy with the machinery of a Greek tragedy. Second, the reader cannot escape the conclusion that the mother has been perfectly willing to see the son die in order to revenge herself on the girl. If we confine ourselves to the probabilities of character as established in the first half of the story, the older woman's act is as incongruous and, from her shrewd point of view, as unnecessary as the load of guilt placed upon the heroine.

The young man's death and the mechanism which caused it are the weak points of the story viewed as a study of character. But in fact they, like very similar developments in the tales of this period, are the indispensable features of the story for James. They represent his effort, relatively crude at this point in his career, to intensify and polarize dramatic conflict. The hero is disposed of not by the girl's

9. James, *The Complete Tales,* I pp. 49-98.

faithlessness or the mother's spite, but rather by Henry James in search of a device to extract from the reader an emotion a good deal more intense than that with which he is likely to view a feckless young girl and a neurotic mother. The action does *not* reveal hitherto unsuspected levels of passionate conflict. Rather it seeks to heighten the prosaic conflict between the two women by suggesting that it is insoluble except through the death of the man they both seek.

The story, written at the beginning of his career, illustrates a general problem James was to face again and again in his work. He sought a means whereby he could achieve from psychological and moral drama an effect, an intensity, which would be at least partially dissipated by a resolution of his action in strict compliance with probabilities of choice characteristic of realistic psychological and moral drama. To have settled for the probable would have meant, among other things, opening himself frankly to the possibility of compromise and adaptation in his characters: most simply, for example, separation for Isabel Archer, marriage for Fleda Vetch, and a career as a political reformer for Hyacinth Robinson. All eminently possible, given the objective facts which we possess about these characters; all equally unthinkable, given what James has made of them by means of his action, his design. Unthinkable, because for James the contingent and problematic solution to a struggle necessarily diminished the evocative power of that struggle.

But if James was unwilling to consign his characters to the probable, he was also unwilling to openly abandon credibility and the appearance of consistency. What results—and it is James's most remarkable achievement—is the creation of an action or situation which manipulates character so as to give it a pathos, heroism, and a dignity unattainable were it left to the resources of its own internal principle of development and forced to adhere to probability. What is remarkable about this achievement is that the position into which a character is manipulated is made to seem most heroic as an expression of his individuality and freedom. The chief characters of "The Story of a Year" *are* allowed to develop throughout the first two-thirds of the story according to the dictates of their personalities, too long for us to accept the device of the son's death. We see it too clearly as an effort to impute to the conflict an intensity and an importance which far outreaches the two personalities. In his mature work James does not allow himself to be caught with such meager resources.

The overt violence and melodramatic effects of the early work were transmuted by James into the imagery of violence which pervades his later work. It was not, I think, simply that James moved from a naive to a sophisticated sense of evil and thereby passed from crude melodrama to moral and psychological tragedy. It was rather that he became at the end of his career a far more serious and successful exploiter of the arts of melodrama, particularly that of a language infused with the rhetoric of violence, its force contained but also intensified by a framework of decorous incidents. This very decorum often concealed violence, of which the typical form in James's fiction is betrayal.

A strategy such as this could serve him better than the overt acts of violence in the early stories. Serve him by awakening in the reader a richer emotion, a stronger sympathy for Isabel and Milly Theale than that which he had been made to experience by the earlier characters. It would be foolish to deny the enormous gain in James's powers of characterization. But the transition from the murder and revenge of the early stories to the image of Charlotte Stant, as a wild beast in *The Golden Bowl,* signals also James's richly increased talent for exploiting within the reader the range of possible reactions to violent conflict.

The American and *Roderick Hudson* find for James's design two contexts which he was also to use throughout his later work: the international theme and the theme of the superiority of artistic consciousness. Christopher Newman turns his back on millions to seek a wife in Europe. The woman he chooses finally accepts him, only to be dispatched to a convent by her mother, who is more willing to suffer the charge of murder than the shame of a commercial son-in-law. The new man and the aging, but still shrewd and sinister aristocracy: "America" and "Europe," two storehouses of cultural myth which, as Christof Wegelin has observed, had been richly supplied by earlier nineteenth-century writers.[10] James used the myths to point the conflict and to orchestrate the reactions of his readers. In his 1907 Preface to *The American* James admitted that the novel was a romance and confessed candidly that he made the Bellegardes implausibly resistant to Newman's wealth. Perhaps not quite so candidly after all, since in the same Preface he delights in Newman's final renunciation of the Bellegarde morality. Newman was born to make this renunciation, to leave Claire in the convent rather than a little of his American purity in Europe, and even the James of 1907 cannot have seriously wished the old countess to spoil the whole

10. Wegelin, *The Image of Europe,* pp. 3-31.

affair by taking Newman and his millions into her family. Without the enduring malice on the part of the Bellegardes, there can be no heroic renunciation by Newman. The implausible malice stays in the revised edition to safeguard Newman's virtue.

Roderick Hudson began as a study of the romantic artist destroyed by impulses which he could not discipline to his art. The character allowed James to internalize violence, make it the function of a spiritual, even an aesthetic condition, rather than a quality of action. But, perhaps uncertain at this point in his development that an aesthetic passion could hold the interest of his reader, he released Roderick and the reader at the end of the novel into convention and violent action: Roderick falls in love with Christina Light and commits suicide. Still, James had opened up what proved to be an immensely attractive theme, congenial to him personally and neatly consistent with his desire for situations rooted in polar conflict: the opposition between the value commonly placed upon act and passion in the observable, social sphere, and the value which James thought to adhere to the solitary passion and choice of the artist. *The Tragic Muse* was James's later, fully developed treatment of this theme.

From the vantage point of 1907, having written *The Tragic Muse* and numerous short stories in which social action or domestic love are openly regarded as both temptation and catastrophe for the artist, James took a less enthusiastic view of Roderick Hudson. He decided, in fact, that Roderick had not been the central figure in the novel which bore his name:

> . . . but I make out in another quarter above all what really saved me. My subject, all blissfully, in face of difficulties, had defined itself—and this in spite of the title of the book—as not directly, in the least, my young sculptor's adventure. This it had been but indirectly, being all the while in essence and in final effect another man's, his friend's and patron's, view and experience of him. . . .
> The centre of interest throughout "Roderick Hudson" is in Rowland Mallet's consciousness, and the drama is the very drama of that consciousness—which I had of course to make sufficiently acute in order to enable it, like a set and lighted scene, to hold the play.[11]

The choice of Rowland Mallet as hero of a novel written thirty-two years before, signals the end of a long development, not just in literary technique, but also in the frankness with which James was willing to acknowledge the basis of his view of experience, as man and writer: the life of observation is now judged to contain a signifi-

11. James, *The Art of the Novel*, pp. 15-16.

cance and an intensity superior to that afforded by sustained involvement in the ordinary business of society. Moreover, the latter is inimical to, in constant conflict with, the former. Action threatens both the form and the intensity of consciousness, threatens to betray it by fragmenting the perfect idea into a series of random facts, and the pleasure of comprehension into one of the several passions for gain.

James denied this dichotomy between action and observation, insisting that the only interest in any drama lay in the capacity of "agents" to comprehend and be moved by what happens to them.

> But there are degrees of feeling—the muffled, faint, the just sufficient, the barely intelligent, as we may say; and the acute, the intense, the complete, in a word—the power to be finely aware and richly responsible. It is those moved in this latter fashion who "get most" out of all that happens to them and who in so doing enable us, as readers of their record, as participators by a fond attention, also to be most.[12]

In practice though, as James developed a technique for increasingly nuanced depiction of the intense consciousness, he lost interest in the specific acts of his central figures and in prosaic motives such as those which animated Basil Ransom, Christopher Newman, and Roderick Hudson. More and more, the role of the central consciousness is to understand and to protect himself against "what happens" in the novel. For the capacity for decisive action is largely given over to characters whose greed and selfishness in contrast with the passions of the observer make action itself in the world of the James novel seem at best hopeless, at worst, evil.

In his autobiography, James finds in the recollected picture of his own boyhood the image of one for whom contemplation had begun to replace action and the kind of assertive involvement in society for which the young Henry's brother, William, already seemed destined.

> What I look back to as my infant license can only have had for its ground some timely conviction on the part of my elders that the only form of riot or revel ever known to me would be that of the visiting mind. Wasn't I myself for that matter even at that time all acutely and yet resignedly, even quite fatalistically, aware of what to think of this? I at any rate watch the small boy dawdle and gape again, I smell the cold dusty paint and iron as the rails of the Eighteenth Street corner rub his contemplative nose, and, feeling him foredoomed, withhold from him no grain of my sympathy. He is a convenient little image or warning of all that was to be for him, and he might well have been even happier than he was. For there was the very pattern and measure of all he was to demand: just to

12. *Ibid.*, p. 62.

be somewhere—almost anywhere would do—and somehow receive an impression or an accession, feel a relation or a vibration. He was to go without many things, ever so many—as all persons do in whom contemplation takes so much the place of action; but everywhere, in the years that came soon after, and that in fact continued long, in the streets of great towns, in New York still for some time, and then for a while in London, in Paris, in Geneva, wherever it might be, he was to enjoy more than anything the so far from showy practice of wondering and dawdling and gaping: he was really, I think, much to profit by it. What it at all appreciably gave him—that is gave him in producible form—would be difficult to state but it seems to him, as he even now thus indulges himself, an education like another: feeling, as he has come to do more and more, that no education avails for the intelligence that doesn't stir in it some subjective passion, and that on the other hand almost anything that does so act is largely educative, however small a figure the process might make in a scheme of training. Strange indeed, furthermore, are some of the things that *have* stirred a subjective passion—stirred it, I mean, in young persons predisposed to a more or less fine inspired application.[13]

James's accounts in his novels of the "education" of consciousness may have their source in some such early decision to profit fully from an observation of life so intense and complete as necessarily to remove him from ordinary action. James did give up a great deal because of this choice; so did his characters, his fine spirits. The burden of much of the rhetoric of his art was to persuade the reader of the value of such a choice. He had, most of all, to imbue the life of observation with the excitement and the moral importance associated, particularly in a secular, vestigially Calvinist culture, with social action. And, most immediately, he needed that basic fictive ingredient without which, he believed, neither the attention nor the allegiance of the reader could be captured: he needed a story, an action or situation which would neatly appropriate to his portrait of consciousness the dramatic intensity of a series of vivid acts. He needed an action for his observer.

One action suited to the dramatic celebration of intense consciousness was the attempt to penetrate some mystery, usually the details and the significance of a particular relationship. Such is the action in *The Sacred Fount* and *The Ambassadors*. Since the concrete events which initiate the relationship are displaced in time, past or future, they can be made to transfer their rhythm and excitement to the movement of the reflective or anticipative consciousness. As the case of Strether makes clear, the consciousness is capable of improv-

13. James, *Small Boy and Others,* pp. 16-17.

ing upon, while being grossly wrong about what really happened. We thus have an action consisting of a variety of incidents, expressions of the desire to know, to discover, sometimes to improve upon reality.

A second type of action, also devised to suit James's rhetorical purposes, was based on the need imposed upon the central consciousness for a choice between two warring parties or principles. Usually such an action begins with the desire on the part of the hero to reconcile the two. Where the opposition is not expressed by persons in direct conflict with one another, it is generated by two neatly contrasting tendencies in the hero himself as, for example, in Nick Dormer of *The Tragic Muse*. Again, Hyacinth Robinson in *The Princess Casamassima* is poised between his longing for revolution and his equally intense longing for all that revolution would destroy.

Fleda Vetch, on the other hand, must choose between loyalty to Mrs. Gereth, tacit approval of her seizure of the "things," and her own conscience, which contents itself at first with a simple insistence that legal obligations be met, however unfair they may be. But what really sustains the novel is James's decision to work out a love relation between Fleda and Owen, in which, for James's particular interests, Owen is to be seen as the human embodiment of the spoils themselves. This makes the choice more difficult for Fleda, of course, but the important thing to note about Fleda's tortured progress from here on is that her love for Owen does not change the essential dilemma: Fleda is still faced with a choice between acquisition and heroic renunciation. She doesn't choose between love and duty; she chooses between a desire to have something and the heroism of being above having.

The interest in *Washington Square* depends much less on the process of choice since Catherine Sloper cannot make choice sufficiently complex to interest James for long. (Hence, the ironic distance between Catherine and the narrator.) In her case she chooses the handsome suitor and is then made to suffer for it. Defeat gives her a certain dignity, but the choice itself, emotional and undistinguished, places her among characters whose frustration James makes inevitable, since they are willing to subordinate consciousness to action.

James frequently animates his characters with motives less specific than the desire to penetrate a mystery or choose between two alternatives. Their strongest impulse is sometimes a generalized "desire to live." The terms of this desire are left purposely vague and usually defined in a negative way (Madame Merle's "young man with the mustaches" emphatically does not satisfy Isabel Archer's dream). The character central to this action usually has no specific intentions, but is moved by the powerful sense that opportunities for an enriched experience have become available as never before in the past. Hope in the hero is awakened or fanned by a sudden dramatic increase in his freedom (as with Isabel's inheritance) or by some special urgency (Milly Theale's sense that she is going to die).

The desire to live is usually associated with Europe, and it is presumed by the Americans that Europe offers opportunities for life not available in the United States. (The chief two *rendered* advantages of Europe are a hierarchical social system and the redolence of the past. The American, having missed the past, can at least put himself into relation with the places which give off vibrations of its evil and splendor.) It is very important that the desire of the heroine be seen as equally vague and intense. By not tying it down, by not being so obvious as to suggest that Isabel comes to be married, Milly to fall in love before she dies, James manages to suggest the full force of a human being's desire to experience. James tries in his stories of this type to achieve a kind of poetic condensation. Take Isabel Archer or Milly Theale, he seems to say. Observe that they have both the means and the ambition for experience. Note the urgency with which they desire to absorb this experience. Take them as types of the general human desire. What is rendered is the distillation of desire, not the particulars of one character's specific hopes and ambitions.

The fourth of James's typical actions is the story of heroes such as Christopher Newman or Basil Ransom, who set out to acquire something, a particular goal. The irony directed by the narrator toward both of these heroes seems calculated partially to deflate the confidence of the man of action in the adequacy of his largely unreflecting acts. And it would seem that in his exclusion of *The Bostonians* from the New York Edition, and in his revisions of *The American,* James was expressing a certain lack of interest in a search limited by such specific goals and desires. We note also that in both works the desired is a wife. In one story, marriage is forsaken in favor of a more satisfying renunciation. In the other, the very last lines of the novel warn us that the marriage which concludes the story is to be far from brilliant.

A fifth type of action, very common in the stories of the middle period, is based on a complex version of the primitive desire for self-protection. In these stories, of which *The Awkward Age* and *What*

Maisie Knew are the best examples, the problem faced by the heroine
is that of protecting herself against and within a corrupt environment.
The heroine is clearly superior, but superior because she refuses to participate in the corrupt actions of those around her. Since there appear
to be no alternatives to corruption except one of several types of
withdrawal, these stories are often static, extended treatments of a situation which does not allow substantial change. Innocence may prevail, but ineffectually; corruption remains as gross as before.

We have established the connection between James's typical
action and his initial conception of character. We have seen that since
the essential drama is that of consciousness, James must generate an
interest and an excitement comparable to that usually associated
with physical, overtly expressed action. Experience which is not
fully "appreciated" by the character is not a fit subject for art, although
it is common enough in life. What makes the "case" for art is the
presence of an intelligence subtle and acute enough to appreciate
its full implications. So that, since a priority has been established,
James's process of selection will operate at least partly to exclude
incidents which, by their violence or fortuitousness, would seem not
to yield their significance to even the most acute observer. And one
cannot help but draw the conclusion from a reading of James's fiction
that to the extent that one *initiates* an action in society, one's appreciation is bound to be less than that of the character who observes
or is primarily affected by the action. The Jamesian protagonist
vibrates most intensely to an action or situation that has been
initiated or structured by someone else.

If the chief character is essentially the victim of action initiated
by others, or involved in a situation for which he is not wholly responsible, who are the characters who initiate? How do they manage it,
and to what effect? We're dealing now with a set of characters whom
James called "fools," whose powers of appreciation are comparatively
feeble, and also with intelligent but aggressive figures like Kate Croy.
Both groups may be located in Richard Poirier's category of the
"fixed character."[14]

We note first of all that if the good characters are recognized
by their willingness to wait for the action to be initiated, the "fools"
are as precisely characterized by the energy of their acts. In general,
they don't participate in the larger movements of the society any
more than do the innocents. But they do act. They sleep with one
another and seize households full of precious objects. They promote

14. Poirier, *The Comic Sense,* pp. 183-246.

and carry off love affairs between their own lovers and wealthy Americans. They milk sentimental gentlemen of their money by putting a price on a daughter's innocence. Most importantly they lay traps for the innocents. And they have considerable power to effect their aims, so long as they do not, as does Mrs. Gereth, depend upon the complicity of the free spirits. Also, their power is limited by their occasional vulnerability to the spiritual influence of the innocent, which, as in the case of Merton Densher, may make new victims of old agents.

The Princess Casamassima offers a good example of the types of vitality available to those not blessed with a fine conscience, whose consciousness is bound by desire. The Princess herself makes use of people to allay the boredom she feels, for in the characters with whom James threatened his innocents, even boredom is capable of generating considerable energy. Paul Muniment, on the other hand, is the narrow ideologue. Stripped of his political trappings, he is the man whose consciousness is so narrowly focused as to make him unfit for anything except action. Once again James insinuates the lesson: in such a milieu the capacity for action is a likely sign of corruption. To be pure is to be paralysed, as is poor Hyacinth. Precisely the same point emerges from a close reading of *The Awkward Age,* with its contrast between Mrs. Brook, whose capacity for action seems directly proportional to her amorality, and Nanda, who is too fine to do anything but love hopelessly, the condition of her love being that it be directed only toward someone who cannot return it.

The action initiated or the situation established by the Jamesian agent is often so ingeniously perverse as to recall the melodrama of the earliest tales. Madame Merle, Kate Croy, and Charlotte Stant all sanction the marriage of a present or former lover to another woman for the purpose of making use of her fortune. Hyacinth Robinson is betrayed by the three people whom he has trusted, the betrayal in each case signaled by a sexual passion which deflects them from what James clearly regarded as their obligation to Hyacinth. Maïsie is trapped in the middle of pairs of adults who will use her in any way to facilitate sexual arrangements they have made or wish to make. Sexual intrigue is a typical motive for the plots which threaten or victimize the protagonist in a James novel. Not only are most of the protagonists presented as relatively asexual— that quality implicitly regarded as a hindrance to the achievement of full consciousness—but also the specific terms of the assault against the free spirit are often sexual.

I have briefly described what seem to me to be the chief features of the Jamesian design incorporated in the action or situation of his novels. That design is of such a nature as to suggest the presence in the author of a commitment prior to, if usually not incompatible with his interest in realistic psychological or moral portraiture. The need for such a design, and the subtlety with which James employed it increased rather than diminished as his interests shifted from overt action to the dynamics of consciousness. The persistence of his design of polar opposition in his later work indicates, as does the violent imagery, a superior exploitation of the evocative powers latent in primitive genres like the melodrama, the legend, and the fairy tale.

But, in order to test my thesis, I should apply it to a work from James's middle period, a period in which he had dropped the overtly violent action of the earliest tales, but still dealt minutely with realistic detail. The question is whether it can be demonstrated that the conception and technique of such a work can be plausibly explained as a result of James's fascination with radical conflict and his desire to stimulate in his reader a comparable fascination. It will be useful to seek an answer to this question in an analysis of the work which has given rise to most speculation about James as a moralist and psychologist: *The Portrait of a Lady.*

2

THE PORTRAIT OF A LADY

Why does Isabel Archer reject Lord Warburton's suit, dismiss Caspar Goodwood, agree to marry Gilbert Osmond, and finally return to him at the end of the novel despite what she now knows of his character? Let us briefly review possible answers supplied by the text. She refuses Warburton because the life he leads and the social system he represents would curtail her freedom.[1] She doubts the sincerity or the distinction of his political ambitions, and hence of the man himself. She honestly believes that she is not "good" enough for him, that is, that her spirit would seem intractable to an English husband trained to expect the ideal of compliance figured in Warburton's sisters. By assuring herself of comfort in a marriage to an English peer, she would weakly evade whatever discomfort or pain her "fate" has in store for her. He threatens the free play of her intelligence.[2] She fears the normal sexual experience that marriage with Warburton would entail.

Goodwood, we may argue, is dismissed for one or more of the

---

1. James, *The Portrait of a Lady*, I, p. 144. Subsequent references are to this edition, volume and page numbers indicated in parentheses after the quotation. The same procedure will be followed after the first reference to other novels of the New York Edition.

following reasons: Isabel recognizes but dislikes *his* personal force, fears the personal, social, or sexual submission it would demand in marriage. He is crude and narrow in his attitudes, insufficiently respectful of her imagination, condescending toward her sex.

Isabel accepts Gilbert Osmond because he seems to be free of systems and artificial conventions and also is disposed to allow his wife a similar freedom. Considered aesthetically, he is perfect, his life an object of beauty. He relieves her of the responsibility of her inheritance. His sexual demands will be minimal. Though disillusioned, she returns to him at the end of the novel through a sense of honor, in fidelity to her promise to Pansy, out of respect for the very institution of marriage, or determination to accept the consequences of her disastrous choice.

The critical problem here is obvious. On the one hand, everything about the Jamesian novel, even the very texture of its prose, warns us against simple formulas. Chapter Six of *The Portrait* pleads not only for sympathy for Isabel but also for a moratorium on the simple psychological and moral judgments we are accustomed to make. To preserve Isabel Archer from "scientific criticism" is to preserve her from the scientist's detachment, but also from his oversimplifications.

Nevertheless, we are committed to the view, fostered by Henry James among others, that whereas life may be confused and contradictory, art is consistent and intelligible, and thus, we edge warily toward a hypothesis that will explain Isabel. We suggest that the dominant impulse in her life, ultimately the cause of her decisions, is her fear of sex, or her desire to retain the American's ideal of freedom, or the need to preserve and extend her intelligence. Other theories have been advanced, but all of them adopt much the same strategy: the location of passage or passages which seem openly to support one's hypothetical central motivation; an effort to demonstrate the consistency and pervasiveness of this motive, even in passages or scenes from which it seems totally absent; the studied neglect or dismissal of parts of the text which resist one's hypothesis.

What I wish to suggest is that this more or less awkward procedure is dictated by a set of related assumptions which may be questionable. The assumptions are as follows: James's primary in-

2. Krook, in *The Ordeal of Consciousness*, pp. 30-1, argues that Lord Warburton's admission that he is afraid of Isabel's mind indicates that after marriage he would attempt to curb the play of that mind. According to Miss Krook, it is because Isabel is unwilling to submit to such restraint that she refuses his offer of marriage.

terest in the novel is the psychological development of Isabel Archer; he accords her such extraordinary freedom so that through her choices she may reveal herself, a complex and "unique" personality; finally, the novel is intended to affect the reader by exhibiting for him *through* Isabel's characterization a given psychological or moral truth (freedom is hazardous, imagination limited, sexual attitudes decisive, and so forth). Now these assumptions may appeal for support to a large body of critical opinion and, although not with complete confidence, to James's own comments in his Preface.[3] What alternatives exist?

I suggest that Isabel ought not to be regarded as an autonomously developed character, the matrix of psychological or moral forces which it is the novel's chief function to illuminate. She ought instead, to be thought of as the principal agent in an action which transports her between the poles of a radical freedom and humiliating submission.

> The idea of the whole thing is that the poor girl, who has dreamed of freedom and nobleness, who has done, as she believes, a generous, natural, clear-sighted thing, finds herself in reality ground in the very mill of the conventional.[4]

The action of *The Portrait of a Lady* is the progressive stages by which Isabel moves from freedom (or her dream of it) to the slavery of marriage with Osmond. That, as James would have said, is the story in it. James may indeed have begun his thought of the novel with only the idea of Isabel, but it appears most likely that integral to this first idea was the polar terms of the action through which Isabel was to travel. That is to say, she may have existed alone in his mind, but she existed even then as a "poor girl," desiring freedom but choosing its opposite. Isabel is given great freedom not chiefly so that she may exhibit or reveal a distinctive personality in her choices, but rather to multiply the author's opportunities to reinforce the central paradox which the whole action of his novel traces: what looks like the highest freedom is perilously close to abject submission. The stages of the action by which James carries his heroine from one to the other of these radical poles of experience is the *design* of the novel. That design is inherent in his conception of Isabel; she exists, in all of her complexity, to serve it. Our response to the novel extends far beyond our perception of Isabel's complexity, our grasp of her "psychology." Above and beyond the fact that the

3. *The Art of the Novel*, pp. 42-8.
4. James, *The Notebooks*, p. 15.

subject of the novel is of great inherent interest, the design of its action exerts a powerful influence upon us. We are surprised into pity by what happens to Isabel, and sobered by the proximity of two conditions we like to think of as manifestly distinct.

The structure of *The Portrait of a Lady* reflects James's effort to exploit his earliest conception of Isabel Archer as the young girl who desires to be free, but who ends by being ground in the mill of the conventional. Equally, the structure, regarded with such satisfaction in the Preface,[5] is a means by which the author protects his heroine from "scientific criticism," and attempts to "awaken on the reader's part an impulse more tender and more purely expectant." (I, 69) James shapes and arranges the parts of his novel to ensure that both Isabel's desire and her suffering will be extraordinary and that we will admire the one and pity the other. James's problem, as he reviewed it in the Preface, was a literary one, partially solved by Shakespeare and George Eliot, evaded by most novelists, Charles Dickens among others: how to make a young woman the plausible heroine of an extended and serious action.

The frail vessel, that charged with George Eliot's "treasure," and thereby of such importance to those who curiously approach it, has likewise possibilities of importance to itself, possibilties which permit of treatment and in fact peculiarly require it from the moment they are considered at all. *There is always the escape from any close account of the weak agent of such spells by using as a bridge for evasion, for retreat and flight, the view of her relation to those surrounding her.* [italics mine] Make it predominately a view of *their* relation and the trick is played: you give the general sense of her effect, and you give it, so far as the raising on it of a superstructure goes, with the maximum of ease. Well, I recall. perfectly how little, in my now quite established connexion, the maximum of ease appealed to me, and how I seemed to get rid of it by an honest transposition of the weights in the two scales. "Place the centre of the subject in the young woman's own consciousness," I said to myself, "and *you get as interesting and as beautiful a difficulty as you could wish.* [italics mine] Stick to *that*—for the centre; put the heaviest weight into *that* scale, which will be largely the scale of her relation to herself. Make her only interested enough, at the same time, in the things that are not herself, and this relation needn't fear to be too limited. Place meanwhile in the other scale the lighter weight (which is usually the one that tips the balance of interest): press least hard, in short, on the consciousness of your heroine's satellites, especially the male; make it an interest contributive only to the greater one. See, at all events, what can be done in this way. What better field could there be for a due ingenuity? The girl hovers, inextinguishable, as a charming crea-

5. *Art of the Novel*, p. 52.

ture, and the job will be to translate her into the highest terms of that formula, and as nearly as possible moreover into *all* of them. To depend upon her and her little concerns wholly to see you through will necessitate, remember, your really 'doing' her."

So far I reasoned, and it took nothing less than that technical rigour, I now easily see, to inspire me with the right confidence for erecting on such a plot of ground the neat and careful and proportioned pile of bricks that arches over it and that was thus to form, constructionally speaking, a literary monument.[6]

The passage I have quoted reveals a considerable similarity between James and the character he created. As Isabel desires to avoid marriage to Warburton and Goodwood, marriage which, however brilliant, would submit her personality to social convention, so also does James wish to escape the conventional literary practice of according to his heroine only such importance as she is able to gain through her relations with the young men around her. Curiously, marriage for Isabel represents almost as great a threat to James's artistic ambitions as it does to Isabel's own sense of possibilities. Marriage to an English lord or an American businessman would subject Isabel and hence her creator to a fate which, if not commonplace, would still not measure up to the as yet rather vague demands of both for the "interesting" and the "beautiful."

Rather than shift the interest from heroine to male satellites, James decides that the chief interest of the novel ought to be Isabel's "relation to herself." This last phrase I take to mean the relation between the young woman and that ideal of herself which she vaguely but intensely maintains throughout the first half of the novel. The prospect of marriage with either Warburton or Goodwood is unsatisfactory for Isabel, precisely because this ideal self derives from her reluctance to accept the relation of marriage as necessarily that which fulfills a woman. Isabel desires this "relation to herself," and her desire comes from, and is analogous to James's wish to center his story in Isabel, rather than in her relations with others. Both Isabel and James tend to assume that the first step toward the distinguished is away from the conventional.

Since the avoidance of marriage is of such concern to both character and author, it is not surprising that Isabel's eventual union with Osmond, a choice which plunges her into the conventional, should be central to the structure of the novel. The division of the novel into two nearly equal parts, the accounts of Isabel before and after her marriage to Osmond, is the chief structural feature of

6. *Ibid.*, pp. 51-2.

the novel. The first half dramatizes Isabel's desire to be free, to remain essentially within that "relation to herself" which James has projected. Here, James explores the possibilities of such freedom and coaxes appreciation from the reader. But Isabel does eventually choose Osmond, and it is one of the most singular achievements of the novel that James contrives to make of that choice the highest expression of the very quality which has distinguished Isabel from the beginning: her desire to achieve distinction *through avoiding* the obvious and the conventional.

But the structure of the novel is not solely a means for dramatizing Isabel's desire to be free. It is also, as I have said, a rhetorical instrument designed to elicit and sustain a feeling "tender and expectant" toward the heroine. For this reason James juxtaposes his treatment of Isabel's freedom with the development of details and motivations which, quite apart from any flaw in Isabel, will operate to thrust her into marriage with Osmond. The two main vehicles here are Ralph's efforts to secure a fortune for Isabel, and Madame Merle's attempt to take advantage of it. We shall later examine the structural importance of Madame Merle's plot as a device by which James controls the reaction of the reader toward Isabel. It is sufficient now to remark that the sinister quality of the plot, as well as the muted presence of the sexually perverse in Madame Merle's motives, direct the sympathy of the reader toward Isabel, make her seem less directly responsible for the choice she makes, and, most importantly, prevent her from seeming to us, at any point in the novel, merely foolish in her decision to marry Gilbert Osmond.

The second half of the novel is a richly detailed treatment of the slavery into which Isabel has fallen, an account of suffering endured by a woman of Isabel's type reduced, not just to conventional marriage, but to marriage with the "very soul of convention." Her relations with Osmond, the dramatized events of their married life, are a carefully intensified version of the ordinary domestic submission which, for Isabel, made distasteful the marriage relation of the period. As James knew, the relation did in fact make a woman important chiefly in relation to her male satellite.

The other important element in the second half of the novel, that which balances James's treatment of Madame Merle's plot in the first half, is the account of Isabel's gradual discovery of what has been done to her. In Chapters Twenty-two to Twenty-nine of the first half, the reader had discovered that Madame Merle was plotting with Osmond to arrange the marriage. In the second half Isabel and the reader discover why, but the effect of the revelation about Osmond and Madame Merle in the second half is to considerably increase our sense of the viciousness of their plot. James must make of his pair something more than conventional fortune hunters, for the lady they bring down is not to be thought of, in her misery, as conventionally deceived. Hence, the bizarre and sordid quality of the plot.

The nature and the probable effects of Isabel's discovery have often been misinterpreted by the critics. It was not James's intention to show Isabel emerging through knowledge out of the sterile marriage with Osmond. She is not going to escape. What we are supposed to conclude, however, is that even as she is ground in the mill of the conventional, she regains something of her original freedom, something of that old relation with her ideal self that she sacrificed in the first part of the novel. She learns the truth about what has been done to her, and she thereby frees herself from the role of submissive wife and ornament of Osmond's salon. Knowledge does not release her from marriage, but it allows her to set for herself the terms and the rationale for remaining within that marriage. She gains the right to cleave to her own somber vision of marriage rather than to Gilbert Osmond. That vision depends upon and is created by the rejuvenated ideal self which her knowledge allows Isabel to partially recover at the end of the novel. A theoretic duty, fidelity to her conception of *herself* as wife, will make divorce as impossible for Isabel as was marriage to Warburton in the first half of the novel. Marriage to Warburton and divorce from Osmond are equally remote from the ideal generated within Isabel's "relation to herself."

To recapitulate, the structure of *The Portrait of a Lady,* particularly the separation of the novel into balanced treatments of Isabel before and after her marriage, precisely reflects James's fascination with the extremes of freedom and submission experienced by Isabel Archer. While making Isabel the agent of an action which passes between these polarities, James ensures that our feelings toward her will be neither harsh nor detached. The second half of the novel balances the portrait of Isabel diminished and miserable with the account of her gradual recovery, through "consciousness," of the means of reentering that "relation to herself" with which the novel begins. We turn now to a more detailed study of James's use of structure to implement his design and control its affective power.

Isabel introduces herself dramatically in the first half of the novel by a series of energetic refusals to do what others expect of her. For the first eight chapters this is her most pronounced note, a fact which becomes clear when we observe how many of her characteristic remarks are declarations of independence from some social or literary formula.

"I don't believe you allow things to be settled for you."
"Oh yes; if they're settled as I like them." (I, 22-3)

"Oh no; she has not adopted me. I'm not a candidate for adoption."
(I, 23)

"Ah," said Isabel slowly, "you must be our crazy Aunt Lydia!"
(I, 32)

"Do everything you tell me? I don't think I can promise that." (I, 35)

. . . Isabel looked disappointed—smiling still, however—and said: "If you please I should like to see them just a little." She was eager, she knew she was eager and now seemed so; she couldn't help it. "She doesn't take suggestions," Ralph said to himself; . . . (I, 61)

"I shall not have success if they're [the English] too stupidly conventional. I'm not in the least stupidly conventional. I'm just the contrary. That's what they won't like." (I, 78-9)

Isabel's cheerful defiance of convention reaches a kind of climax in Chapter Seven when Mrs. Touchett finds it necessary to instruct Isabel in the proprieties of receiving an English lord:

"But I always want to know the things one shouldn't do."
"So as to do them?" asked her aunt.
"So as to choose," said Isabel. (I, 93)

The Isabel of these first eight chapters impresses the other characters as a young woman fiercely, if often theoretically, determined not to do what is expected of her (as young woman, poor niece, visiting American) unless and until these expectations receive the superior sanction of her own will. Moreover, the construction of this section secures for Isabel's essentially negative freedom the admiration of the reader, and checks what otherwise might be our tendency to dismiss her as simply willful. This is managed, first of all, by introducing us to Isabel's assertiveness in the context of Gardencourt, an environment which stands badly in need of energy. Enough has been written by the critics, most notably Richard Poirier,[7] to convince us of the success with which James, in the first two chapters of the novel, has sketched the comfort, the civilization, and the warmth of Daniel Touchett's country home. But too little has been said about the distinct note of lassitude and passivity which the

7. *The Comic Sense,* pp. 190-95.

actors, significantly all three men, contribute to the scene. Mr.
Touchett is an invalid, Ralph, although clever, is sick; and Warburton
amuses himself with indecision.

> "I quite agree with you, sir," Lord Warburton declared. "I'm very sure
> there will be great changes, and that all sorts of queer things will happen.
> That's why I find so much difficulty in applying your advice; you know
> you told me the other day that I ought to 'take hold' of something. One
> hesitates to take hold of a thing that may the next moment be knocked
> skyhigh." (I, 11)

Ralph immediately recommends to Warburton that he "take hold
of a pretty woman," and several moments later when Isabel arrives
all three men stir themselves to follow the advice.

Isabel may be young, naive, stubborn, intemperate; she may
have all the defects which the narrator admits in Chapter Six, but
the fact is that the three characters who, by James's construction,
preside over the world of the novel before Isabel makes her appearance cannot do more than yawn, take care of one another's infirmities,
and make charmingly desultory conversation. They need Isabel
Archer as always in the fables which James devised the cultivated
Europe needed America's energy; and the dramatized need for some
force strong enough to disturb the perfection and the listlessness of
that late afternoon at Gardencourt shields Isabel from criticism in her
repeated refusals to accept what this world chooses to expect of her.
Better energetic conceit than the murmured solicitudes of Ralph and
the perfection of Lord Warburton's riding costume. We have a
choice, and the terms of that choice, laid down through the scene
in Daniel Touchett's garden, make us protective toward Isabel because of her assertiveness. By introducing his heroine into such a
milieu James says in effect: take note of her presumption if you
will, but admit at the same time that it is considerably more vital
than the order on which it presumes.

At the same time, the treatment of Mrs. Touchett and Henrietta
Stackpole also frames and protects Isabel's egotism from undue criticism. Both women are energetic; both judge by theories which are
extensions of their own personalities. Both function as crude simpli-
fications of tendencies in Isabel's own character. They scorn English
society, for quite different reasons, of course, and both are in
rebellion against contemporary standards of wifely or feminine duty.
Isabel is like and likes both women, and James makes this perfectly
plain at various points in the text. What clearly distinguishes Isabel
from both is the heroine's intense but vague ambition. (Henrietta

is ambitious, but in anything but a vague way. She wants to cover Europe for the *New York Interviewer,* a fact which is made sufficiently comic in its precise finality to distract us from the thought that Isabel wants to appropriate the same territory, for her soul rather than for the *Interviewer.*)

In contrast to the men at Gardencourt Isabel is vital, energetic in her self-confidence. In contrast to Mrs. Touchett and Henrietta, the other energetic women who frame Isabel in the novel, she is not narrow or restricted by precise ambition. The structure of the first section of the novel, while providing us, in Chapter Six, with the admission of Isabel's weaknesses, still conspires to produce in the reader an acceptance, perhaps even admiration for her two most prominent faults: her "desire to think well of herself," and her capacity for intensely vague ambition.

James draws upon and extends this admiration in his management of Isabel's refusal of her two suitors. We have already observed Isabel in the process of making a series of essentially negative choices, that is, refusing to follow formulas devised for young women of her situation. The offers of marriage from Warburton and Goodwood must be made to seem increasingly attractive but not essentially dissimilar temptations to sacrifice her ambition for the sake of the ordered and the predictable. Isabel will refuse, but as for her reasons for doing so, her motivation, James has reasons for avoiding perfect clarity. Specification limits the range of her freedom. The principle here is precisely the one invoked by James in his treatment of evil, particularly in the ghost stories of the nineties. Precise and exact specification of a phenomenon or of an emotion sets limits upon its affective force.[8] Therefore, in order that we will be struck more by Isabel's freedom itself than by either the source or the specific end of that desire, James offers us a variety of *possible* explanations, rather than one definite reason, for Isabel's refusals.

Each of these explanations has a certain plausibility; moreover, the author goes to the trouble of offering to the reader, prior to Warburton's proposal, dramatized insights into aspects of his character which make him less desirable than he might otherwise have appeared. So that the reader might fashion for himself, independent of the various reasons used by Isabel, a *pretext* for her dissatisfaction with Warburton, James gives us scenes in which his political serious-

---

8. Preface to *The Aspern Papers, The Art of the Novel,* pp. 175-76. James is discussing the treatment of Peter Quint and Miss Jessel in *The Turn of the Screw.*

ness is questioned and his actual attitude toward women gently satirized.[9]

Warburton's politics and his treatment of the women in his household make Isabel's objection to the "system" which his life entails a plausible pretext for her decision. The lord's sisters work against him so far as Isabel and the reader are concerned, and the same may be said for Henrietta Stackpole's blunt advocacy of Goodwood's suit. It is easy enough in retrospect to say that Isabel ought to be intelligent enough to separate the two men from the women who advertise their virtues, but James has so cleverly planned this section of the novel as to bring the reader under the same, unspoken intuition: quite apart from objections to the men themselves, it is clear that Isabel, once again in her pride and her vagueness, is superior to Henrietta and to the Misses Molyneux. Doubts about the success of a possible relation between Isabel and either of the two men are subtly implanted in the action by a dramatization of the relations which already exist between the two and young women. And again, James works his effects upon the reader without definitely committing himself or his heroine to a single, precise explanation for her refusals. We are merely allowed to sense the plausibility of Isabel's decision, and admire the passion and the consistency with which she maintains her desire to be free, even in the face of such splendid bribes.

In Chapters Ten through Sixteen James combines the two courtships of his heroine. Caspar's letter, reminding Isabel of the encouragement she has given him, arrives in Chapter Eleven. In the same chapter Henrietta speaks out as Goodwood's self-appointed emissary, and in the chapter that follows Lord Warburton proposes. He appears, in fact, just after Isabel has finished reading Goodwood's letter. In Chapter Thirteen Isabel explains her refusal of Warburton to Mr. Touchett, mentally resolves to reject Goodwood, and composes a letter of refusal to Lord Warburton. In the next chapter she has her last interview with Warburton, tries to explain to him the reasons for her decision. In Chapter Fifteen it is Ralph to whom she makes her explanation, and in Chapter Sixteen James gives us, in a violent scene in Isabel's London hotel room, her meeting with and rejection of Caspar Goodwood.

Two strategies become clear from a consideration of the struc-

---

9. Both effects are achieved in the scene in Chapter Nine in which Isabel flusters the two Misses Molyneux with questions about their "radical" brother's political sincerity. (I, 105-08).

ture of these six chapters. First, the two proposals and the rejections which they call forth are treated almost simultaneously. No one in the novel remarks this, but it is as though Isabel, who we know has frightened the men of New York so that she has not been unduly bothered with proposals in the past, is suddenly besieged by offers. Also, the characters of Warburton and Goodwood seem carefully devised and exhibited here in these chapters to convey the full force of masculine attractiveness, that is, in James's scheme of things, the widest range of temptation to a young woman of Isabel's situation to quit that situation in favor of marriage. Warburton incorporates the high cultivation, ease, and charm of the English aristocracy; while Goodwood represents the dynamism and compelling force of American business. "Represent" is not used here to deny either of the two men a distinct identity and a thoroughly plausible personality of their own. It is simply that in the management of these two at this point in the novel James stresses their emblematic role. This for the purpose of emphasizing the distinction of Isabel's refusal to be tempted by that which was generally supposed most desirable to young women of her situation. To juxtapose the appeals of the two men is to stress the energy with which Isabel is prepared to foster her freedom, and to diminish the problem of motivation, the obdurate why does she choose as she does? which so often deflects the attention of the critic. Unless we force ourselves free of the context of this part of the novel, such a question is likely to get lost, as James intended it to, in our attention to and admiration for Isabel's determination.

The second of the two structural devices by which James organizes this section of the novel establishes a rhythm which dominates the whole book. This rhythm we might call a pattern of retrospection, and it is used to ensure that Isabel, unlike the heroine of most novels of the period, will dominate the action in which she is involved. We see the pattern at work in Chapters Thirteen to Sixteen, in those scenes in which Isabel reflects on and justifies—the two processes are in fact inseparable—a choice she has made. James reaches the climax of this rhythm in Chapter Forty-two, but, as he pointed out in his Preface, it is characteristic of the whole book.[10] The scenes show Isabel trying to exercise over her experience a degree of control and authority which she cannot hope to achieve in the act itself. The persistence of such scenes dramatizes Isabel's characteristic attitude, her refusal to submit to the obvious and the

10. *The Art*, p. 57.

conventional, her negative freedom. She wants not so much to turn her mind and her consciousness to future experience in order that it might be controlled, but rather to shape the past in order that it might conform to her ideal of herself. Deep in Isabel Archer is this desire, abetted by James's decision to center the novel in her consciousness, to ignore or rationalize the past for the sake of bringing it into conformity with her ideal of herself. Her refusal to submit to experience herself, to let it be what it is, is what distinguishes her for James as the young woman who wants to be free.

Chapter Sixteen concludes with Isabel's violent rejection of Goodwood, a rejection made imperious by the businessman's conviction that Isabel has little choice but to marry. Goodwood speaks for the male of his day and also for the contemporary novelist. Isabel speaks for the self which has defined itself through heroic refusals of the expected, but also for James the author, committed to treatment of a heroine capable of dominating our attention in her own right.

> "An unmarried woman—a girl of your age—isn't independent. There are all sorts of things she can't do. She's hampered at every step."
> "That's as she looks at the question," Isabel answered with much spirit. "I'm not in my first youth—I can do what I choose—I belong quite to the independent class. I've neither father nor mother; I'm poor and of a serious disposition; I'm not pretty. I therefore am not bound to be timid and conventional; indeed I can't afford such luxuries. Besides, I try to judge things for myself; to judge wrong, I think, is more honourable than not to judge at all. I don't wish to be a mere sheep in the flock; I wish to choose my fate and know something of human affairs beyond what other people think it compatible with propriety to tell me." She paused a moment, but not long enough for her companion to reply. He was apparently on the point of doing so when she went on: "Let me say this to you, Mr. Goodwood. You're so kind as to speak of being afraid of my marrying. If you should hear a rumour that I'm on the point of doing so—girls are liable to have such things said about them— remember what I have told you about my love of liberty and venture to doubt it." (I, 228-29)

The speech is a small masterpiece of Jamesian rhetoric in support of the idea of negative freedom: Isabel speaks of the distinction and the freedom available to her by virtue of what she lacks; her love of liberty expresses itself in refusal; her self-esteem resides in her sense of judging for herself, which act makes even error a source of satisfaction. This is Isabel at her most triumphant, exulting in victory over Goodwood and the insistent masculinity which he represents. So exhilarated is she at having escaped the twin systems of an English lord and an American businessman, that she cannot take seriously the question put forth by a comically sober Henrietta Stackpole: "Do you know where you're drifting?"

"No, I haven't the least idea, and I find it very pleasant not to know. A swift carriage, of a dark night, rattling with four horses over roads that one can't see—that's my idea of happiness." (I, 235)

Isabel's imagination is, as James has pointed out in Chapter Six, sometimes ridiculously overactive, and she is frequently disposed to take such romantic daydreams more seriously than she does in this conversation. But the remark, glib as it is, indicates something important about Isabel's state of mind and about the direction in which James will turn his novel from this point (Chapter Seventeen).

Isabel's rejection of Warburton and Goodwood has temporarily exhausted the possibilities of freedom available to James's heroine. She has climaxed her persistent refusal to be bound by the expected in her long speech to Goodwood. But Isabel will have to be made to choose eventually, for the evocative power of her negative freedom and her immense ambition is not limitless. What has been developed up to this point in the novel is a rich expectancy, a sense in the reader that such splendid refusals of convention must issue in a concrete choice of great value. But the decision to accept someone or some course of action is a hazardous one for both James and Isabel. To accept would be to submit oneself to the particular, to resign oneself to dealing with the precise contingencies of marriage, a friendship, a specific course of action. It would be, necessarily, to relinquish some of the energy and the certitude, the self-assurance which has characterized all of Isabel's decisions to this point. It would be, finally, to penetrate that aura of vague magnificence with which James has nourished Isabel's desire to "live," to learn something about life, to see.

James's solution to the problem comes much closer to Isabel's "swift carriage, of a dark night" than has been generally recognized. The solution was to shift the focus enough away from the heroine to enable James to develop a situation in which the full responsibility for Isabel's eventual choice would not have to be borne solely or even primarily by the heroine herself. Instead, she would be made to suffer, in full measure, the effects of a choice which was partly determined for her. True, Isabel chooses an Osmond whom she herself has created in her imagination, in defiance of the world's opinion. But James, to save her from the criticism which such an act might arouse in the reader, *gives* her an Osmond also created by a sinister plot, a discarded mistress' hopes for her illegitimate daughter, a fortune hunter's greed. In short, James contrives to allow Isabel to escape the full responsibility, but not the suffering, for her naiveté, her stubborn pride. He gives her a coach and a dark night in which to be driven to her marriage with Osmond.

In Chapters Eighteen and Nineteen Isabel appears to have been given a momentary rest from choice and the claims of others. She returns from London to Gardencourt with Ralph to wait sadly for the death of his father. She meets Madame Merle, hesitates only momentarily before deciding that she is charmed by her. But what looks like a period of calm for Isabel is actually the first unobtrusive movement of circumstances out of her control and her consciousness. From this point until Isabel learns the truth about Madame Merle and Osmond, the novel is dominated by Madame Merle's plot, although the point of view remains chiefly with Isabel.

In Chapter Eighteen, Ralph, like James himself admiring and wishing to pay tribute to the American girl, secures a fortune for Isabel. Madame Merle, who will dispose of this fortune, appears in the very next chapter. Chapters Twenty and Twenty-one move Isabel to Europe, carry her through the initial shock of finding herself suddenly an heiress, and ensure the reader that Isabel will not, like the American expatriates Mr. and Mrs. Luce, establish herself in Paris to buy a predictable and socially sanctioned type of unreality. Though the shock of inheritance is severe, she regains her composure and her fortune becomes "to her mind a part of her better self; . . ." (I, 321-22) Like Isabel's power to marry, the money increases its value as Isabel refuses to use it in conventional ways. But, again like her power to marry, the seventy thousand pounds makes her terribly vulnerable to someone astute enough to realize that Isabel's "ideal self" defines itself in avoidance of the ordinary, but beyond this, hardly at all. Ralph thinks that by giving her money he is "put[ting] a little wind in her sails," but quite the contrary is true. He weighs her down with gold which must be spent in order to have meaning. And it is in the spending, the decision to take rather than to forgo, that Isabel is most weak and vulnerable. Things, as she puts it to Madame Merle, do not express her, and the unwillingness to allow herself to be expressed by the *taking* of a thing lays her open to exploitation by predators, to whom, in James, things are liable to be wholly expressive.

Between Chapter Twenty-two, when we are given the first scene in Osmond's house, and Chapter Twenty-nine, when Osmond proposes, the reader is pulled far ahead of Isabel in his understanding of the developing situation. We know that Madame Merle has conceived a plan to marry Isabel to Gilbert Osmond after learning of the American girl's fortune. We know that Osmond and Madame Merle are intimate enough to develop their plan openly between themselves, discussing the advantages and disadvantages of various kinds of strategy. We observe—for the narrator directs us quite pointedly— the indolence and self-absorption of Osmond, and the shrewdness with which Madame Merle is prepared to exploit Isabel.

We have noted earlier the key structural significance of Isabel's declarations of negative freedom, culminating in her refusal of Goodwood. The third major section of the novel, which shifts the action (and for the most part the point of view) from Isabel and freedom to Madame Merle's exercise in active manipulation, unfolds by means of a series of increasingly sinister conversations behind the heroine's back. Such conversations increase the reader's foreboding, impress us with Madame Merle's cleverness, and ultimately shield Isabel from censure for stupidity. Most of all, they revive action, the possibilities for which have been temporarily exhausted by Isabel's climactic refusal. The following excerpts typify the manner in which James allows this section of the novel to be subtly controlled by the atmosphere and the rhetoric of melodrama, the tonal and structural counterpart to Isabel's brilliant declarations on her own liberty.

"There's a friend of mine I want you to know . . ."
"What good will it do me?" he asked with a sort of genial crudity.
Madame Merle waited, "It will amuse you." (I, 343)

"Resist us? Why do you [the Countess Gemini] express yourself so coarsely? She's not exposed to compulsion or deception."
"I'm not sure of that. You're capable of anything, you [Madame Merle] and Osmond. I don't mean Osmond by himself, and I don't mean you by yourself. But together you're dangerous — like some chemical combination." (I, 386)

"You who know everything," Mrs. Touchett said, "you must know this: whether that curious creature's really making love to my niece."
"Gilbert Osmond?" Madame Merle widened her clear eyes and, with a full intelligence, "Heaven help us," she exclaimed, "that's an idea!" (I, 396)

"The girl's not disagreeable," Osmond quietly conceded.
Madame Merle dropped her eye on him a moment, during which her lips closed with a certain firmness. "Is that all you can find to say about that fine creature?"
"All? Isn't it enough? Of how many people have you heard me say more?"

She made no answer to this, but still presented her talkative grace to the room. "You're unfathomable," she murmured at last. "I'm frightened at the abyss into which I shall have cast her." (I, 411)

The heroine is warned of the danger by her own perceptions, but these she turns aside. The major effect, however, of the portrait of Isabel at this stage is not that of a woman misjudging, but rather of a woman betrayed by the deceit of a very shrewd antagonist, who yet comes close to penetrating the scheme. Not merely by giving us more information than Isabel possesses, but by subjecting the reader himself to the ominous atmosphere of Madame Merle's plot, James makes it very difficult for us to withhold sympathy from Isabel, threatened apparently by so much more than an unworthy suitor.

Only after James has thoroughly established the sinister and subtly coercive nature of Madame Merle's plot does he turn his attention to dramatizing Isabel's decision. This he manages in a series of scenes beginning in Chapter Thirty-two, after a two-chapter pause in the action, a foreshortened account of about a year which Isabel spends touring Asia and visiting with her sister. In these two chapters almost nothing is said about Isabel's reaction to Osmond's proposal, or about the decision which, we later learn, she is in the process of making.

The omission is a strategic one and it has considerable significance rhetorically, for it operates to sustain in the mind of the reader precisely the impression of Isabel which James wishes us to entertain. James did not wish to dramatize the *process* by which Isabel arrives at her decision to marry Gilbert Osmond. He allows her to defend that decision in confrontations with Goodwood, Mrs. Touchett, and finally Ralph, but this comes later in the novel after she has, in her own mind, committed herself irrevocably to her choice. And James will allow her, especially in the celebrated Chapter Forty-two, to examine her decision in retrospect. But about the crucial process of choice, the only time in the novel, after all, when Isabel Archer makes up her mind to take rather than to reject or renounce, James is largely silent.

Isabel defends her decision, defends it in a series of dramatic confrontations which, as we shall see, extend to its furthest limits the affective power of her negative freedom. Against the arguments posed by her friends, arguments which incorporate the full range of social, psychological, and moral inducements *against* marriage with Osmond, Isabel poses her own will, and the right of that will to create the object which it chooses. If we stand back from the context and view her decision objectively, Isabel is simply wrong. But the structure of the novel subordinates our sense of her error to our much stronger impression of the extravagant deception of which she is victim. Secondly, James so contrives the series of dramatic confrontations between Isabel and her friends as to place Goodwood, Mrs. Touchett, and Ralph subtly in a false position. In effect, they require of Isabel that she curb the very qualities which have before made her so desirable to them all. All of them ask of her that she submit her splendid self-esteem and her vague ambition to the dictates of common sense. Not an unreasonable request, but then it was not for her common sense that she was taken up by any of the three who now invoke the principle.

Consider, for example, the light in which James's treatment of the interview places Caspar Goodwood.

> "Who and what then is Mr. Gilbert Osmond?"
> "Who and what? Nobody and nothing but a very good and very honourable man. He's not in business," said Isabel. "He's not rich; he's not known for anything in particular."
> ..."Where does he come from? Where does he belong?"
> ..."He comes from nowhere. He has spent most of his life in Italy."
> "You said in your letter he was American. Hasn't he a native place?"
> . . . .
> "What has he ever done?" he added abruptly.
> "That I should marry him? Nothing at all," Isabel replied while her patience helped itself by turning a little to hardness. "If he had done great things would you forgive me any better? Give me up, Mr. Goodwood; . . ." (II, 46-7)

Goodwood is anything but disinterested, but apart from this his criticism of Osmond is, for Isabel at least, an appeal to criteria which Isabel has been at pains to deny since she first entered the novel, criteria which also had little to do with her former interest in Goodwood himself. Isabel may not have been comfortable or confident as she meditated by herself on Osmond's proposal, but this hesitation James conceals from the reader. She is perfectly comfortable when embattled in defense of her right to choose a husband without enquiring who he is, where he comes from, or whether he has a native place. Mrs. Touchett, in the chapter immediately following, continues to refer Isabel to the type of conventional wisdom against which she has always struggled, with the sympathy and, largely, the support of the reader.

> "[Osmond] has no money; he has no name; he has no importance. I value such things and I have the courage to say it; I think they're very precious. Many other people think the same, and they show it. But they give some other reason." (II, 55)

Ralph cares more for Isabel than does his mother; his concern over her marriage to a man he thinks unworthy is difficult for Isabel to dismiss as either interested or conventional. But when Ralph, unable to control himself, calls Osmond a "sterile dilettante," he, no less than Goodwood and Mrs. Touchett, is attacking more than the individual Gilbert Osmond. He attacks, by trying to curb, that very freedom of Isabel's which James has developed consistently from the beginning of the novel. Isabel *has* been consistent throughout. She has chosen with the sense that the ordinary benefits of life are not likely to satisfy her, and her major acts have been refusals to accept the ordinary. Her ambitions have been vague, and those around her, particularly Ralph, have applauded and indeed invested in these ambitions. For her, Gilbert Osmond is both a man closest to herself in his refusal to accept the ordinary, and in the value which she places in negative freedom, the creation of her own passionate will to be free.

> "Your mother has never forgiven me for not having come to a better understanding with Lord Warburton, and she's horrified at my contenting myself with a person who has none of his great advantages—no property, no title, no honours, no houses, nor lands, nor position, nor reputation, nor brilliant belongings of any sort. It's the total absence of all these things that pleases me. Mr. Osmond's simply a very lonely, a very cultivated and a very honest man—he's not a prodigious proprietor." (II, 74)

It is, as James remarks in the passage which follows, "wonderfully characteristic of [Isabel] that, having invented a fine theory about Gilbert Osmond, she loved him not for what he really possessed, but for his very poverties dressed out as honours." (II, 75) But equally, it is wonderfully characteristic of James that Isabel's desire to be free, dramatically expressed by her refusal to become "adopted," the wife of a lord, one of "the companions of freemen," the expatriate heiress, any of the roles which her situation offers, should choose a husband whose value eludes any standard but that of her own will. In choosing him she is finally free from social and moral systems which have some objective existence outside of that fertile "relation with herself," which James has sketched from the beginning of the novel.

> The discreet opposition offered to her marriage by her aunt and her cousin made on the whole no great impression upon her; the moral of it was simply that they disliked Gilbert Osmond. This dislike was not alarming to Isabel; she scarcely even regretted it; for it served mainly to throw into higher relief the fact, in every way so honourable, that she married to please herself. (II, 77)

The first half of the novel ends with Isabel determined to marry to please herself. The movement of this half has been designed to present us with increasingly dramatic, increasingly vivid portraits of the woman who "has dreamed of freedom." James wishes to focus as much as possible on the consciousness of the heroine, to avoid shifting the interest to her male satellite. Both Isabel's desire to be free and her ambitions for experience are, in James's judgment, most intense and evocative when least specific; the choice of a particular course of action diminishes our sense of what is *possible* for Isabel. No such diminution occurs so long as James makes her freedom, in operation, essentially negative. But eventually the specific choice must be made, since James cannot completely evade the conventions of nineteenth-century fiction (which dictate that the point of marriageable young women is that they marry) or the broader demands of the myth with which he has held his reader: the hero or heroine must eventually stake his strength in action.

Isabel chooses Osmond, a character who is designed first of all to impose upon her the misery which is one-half the polar design of James's original concept. Thus, we first see him as devious, indolent, selfish in the extreme. But also, James's decision to dramatize not the process by which Isabel makes her choice, but rather the defiant justification of that choice against the strictures of common sense makes the decision to marry Osmond the most extravagant, even heroic, expression of the freedom which Isabel has typified since she appeared at Gardencourt.

James's intention, according to his notebook entry for *The Portrait of a Lady,* was to develop in the second half of the book the situation "established by Isabel's marriage." It is at this point in his entry that he reminds himself that "the idea of the whole thing is that the poor girl, who has dreamed of freedom and nobleness, who has done, as she believes, a generous, natural, clear-sighted thing, finds herself in reality ground in the very mill of the conventional."[11] The structure of the first half of the novel was designed as a series of increasingly vivid, increasingly interesting demonstrations of Isabel's desire to be free; the second half will consist of similarly gradated versions of the misery she now suffers, ground in the mill of the conventional.

After witholding Isabel from the reader in the first chapter—three years have passed and Ned Rosier has reappeared, hoping to marry Pansy Osmond—James lets us see her in Osmond's drawing room,

11. *The Notebooks,* p. 15.

framed by Rosier's point of view and Osmond's gilded doorway:

> She had lost something of that quick eagerness to which her husband had privately taken exception—she had more of the air of being able to wait. Now, at all events, framed in the gilded doorway, she struck our young man as the picture of a gracious lady. (II, 105)

Losing her eagerness, she has become the picture of a gracious lady. A lady who, in this same interview with the exceedingly eager Ned Rosier, has adapted herself to the reality of the social order more successfully than it would have seemed possible for the Isabel Archer of the first part of the book:

> Poor Rosier gazed at her half-pleadingly, half-angrily; a sudden flush testified to his sense of injury. "I've never been treated so," he said. "What is there against me, after all? That's not the way I'm usually considered. I could have married twenty times."
> "It's a pity you didn't. I don't mean twenty times, but once, comfortably," Isabel added, smiling kindly. "You're not rich enough for Pansy." (II, 117)

And if the Isabel who appeared at Gardencourt seemed intensely, if naively conscious of her own powers, this Isabel seems equally passionate in her conviction of limitation. Rosier attempts an apology for his impetuousness:

> "I referred to Mr. Osmond as I shouldn't have done, a while ago," he began. "But you must remember my situation."
> "I don't remember what you said," she answered coldly.
> "Ah, you're offended, and now you'll never help me."
> She was silent an instant, and then with a change of tone: "It's not that I won't; I simply can't!" Her manner was almost passionate. (II, 117-18)

The interview from which these excerpts are taken occurs in Chapter Thirty-seven. Isabel's deference to social formula and her expression of helplessness are but the first dramatic indications of her misery, the first unfolding of the situation established by her marriage. Still, the picture of Isabel here presented stands in powerful contrast to our last sight of her in the first part of the novel: her extraordinary defense of her choice of Osmond. In these two scenes, centrally located in the structure of *The Portrait,* James represents his design.

A part of Isabel's new function as representative of Gilbert Osmond, presiding over his salon, is to contribute to the elegantly insincere tone which is Osmond's standard of social intercourse:

> "You see the fame of your Thursdays has spread to England," Osmond remarked to his wife.

"It's very kind of Lord Warburton to come so soon; we're greatly flattered," Isabel said.

"Ah well, it's better than stopping in one of those horrible inns," Osmond went on. (II, 124)

"We're greatly flattered" neatly counterpoints "the fame of your Thursdays," in a rhythm to which Isabel has apparently become well accustomed by now. There are a number of such touches in her speech, and their cumulative effect is important. When we consider that a major part of Isabel's freedom and her beauty in the first section of the novel was the perfect correspondence between her outward manner and her thoughts and feelings, even the occasional lapse into the acquired facility of Osmond's tone indicates something important about Isabel's situation. Either she herself has been infected with something of the artificiality of her husband, or, what is more likely in the light of the direction the story is to take, we are to suppose her drugged into a kind of submissiveness, or sleep, in which the falseness of her imitation does not really strike her.

A sleep into which his heroine had fallen was in fact, the image which James himself used in his notebook entry when describing what he wanted to make of the second half of the novel:

> Isabel wakes from her sweet delusion—oh, the art required for making this delusion natural! — and finds herself face to face with a husband who has ended by conceiving a hatred for her own larger qualities.[12]

The dream into which Isabel seems to have fallen and from which she will awake in this second half of the novel is one of the conventions employed by James to achieve a structure more suitable to his idea of intense, polar opposition than to the cumulative and problematic movement of psychological or moral fiction. Instead of following Isabel through the slow, painful stages of her disillusionment (or the process by which the decision was made), we are presented with the heroine only after relations with her husband have completely deteriorated. She is but asleep, captive of Osmond's influence and, as the imagery suggests, imprisoned within the house furnished by her fortune. Her misery is an accomplished fact for the reader, not the consequence of a series of observed developments in the relations between husband and wife. She awakes in the second half of the novel to discover what has been done to her, and the revelations of the Countess Gemini, as well as the sinister imagery of Chapter Forty-two, forcibly prevent us from losing sight of Isabel as the victim of a scheme

12. *Ibid.*

about which she could have had no foreknowledge. We are not allowed to see her merely as a young woman who has made a terrible error in judging her future husband's character.

Rosier's suit of Pansy Osmond is first of all a device for awakening Isabel from her sleep of submission to her husband. About his passion there is always something faintly comic, but so was there a humorous note to Isabel's enthusiasm in the first scenes in which she appeared. Rosier's appearance compels Isabel to recognize that this passion which makes the young man lurk in doorways and rush off to sell his collection of lace is qualitatively different from the emotions with which Osmond views marriage, whether that of his daughter or his own. And since Osmond intends that Isabel should discourage the young man and actively encourage Lord Warburton to take Pansy, Rosier's suit forces into the open the antagonism between Isabel's nature and that of her husband. Rosier's function in the plot, his role as the young man who braves the cold and sterile atmosphere of Osmond's castle for the sake of passion, suggests the fairy tale figure of the youth who awakens the princess from the sleep into which she has fallen, a role more suitable for Goodwood had James intended to allow Isabel to break away, finally and definitively, from the submission into which she has fallen. Since he intends her emergence to be into knowledge but to stop short of act, James provides Rosier, who awakens Isabel with his awkward but genuine love for Pansy.

But James's use of Rosier in the action of *The Portrait* is not confined to his emblematic role. The development in which he involves Isabel, against her will, reveals more to the reader about the humiliation forced upon her by her marriage. Wishing to please Osmond even at this point, Isabel agrees that a match with Lord Warburton is far more desirable for Pansy than one with the less brilliant Ned Rosier.

> It would please [Osmond] greatly to see Pansy married to an English nobleman, and justly please him, since this nobleman was so sound a character. It seemed to Isabel that if she could make it her duty to bring about such an event she should play the part of a good wife. (II, 174)

She acts to further the match, at least to the point of encouraging Pansy to notice Warburton's qualities and to be dutiful to her father's wishes. Only when she realizes that Warburton is motivated by a desire to draw closer to her by marrying her stepdaughter, does Isabel act to discourage the match. Her discouragement of Warburton, although effective, is very indirect, as though Isabel wished scrupulously to avoid disloyalty to Osmond and James was unwilling to allow his heroine to rebel except in circumstances that could not possibly bring discredit on her. Moreover, Isabel does for a period of time try to please Osmond by furthering the match and by doing so gives us another measure of the situation into which her marriage has forced her. Her manner becomes necessarily similar to that of Madame Merle and in retrospect the reader perceives that Isabel unwittingly approaches the role acted out by the older woman in the first half of the novel: that of arranging a marriage between a former lover and a young woman for the sake of pleasing Gilbert Osmond.

Osmond makes it clear to Isabel that he expects her to use her influence with Warburton to bring about the marriage. Immediately following this scene is Chapter Forty-two, which contains Isabel's shocked recognition of her situation. The chapter and the emotional process it dramatizes are complex and have received major emphasis in all extended critical treatments of the novel. Indeed, the chapter has perhaps received too much attention, for it has begun to seem a kind of *tour de force,* the "best thing in the book," and for this reason separable from its context. This is not so. The scene is important as a part of the development of James's design and his rhetorical strategy for guiding the response of the reader. Isabel for the first time in the novel directly confronts the misery of her marriage, signs of which misery the reader has observed, steadily intensified, in each scene since Chapter Thirty-seven, when Isabel, now Mrs. Osmond, reentered the story. Through Isabel's mind in this chapter play the images of captivity and of the evil of her husband's nature, imagery which internalizes the conventions of the Gothic tale and hence obviates the need for more overtly melodramatic development of the plot.

> She could live it over again, the incredulous terror with which she had taken the measure of her dwelling. Between those four walls she had lived ever since; they were to surround her for the rest of her life. It was the house of darkness, the house of dumbness, the house of suffocation. Osmond's beautiful mind gave it neither light nor air; Osmond's beautiful mind indeed seemed to peep down from a small high window and mock at her. Of course it had not been physical suffering; for physical suffering there might have been a remedy. She could come and go; she had her liberty; her husband was perfectly polite. He took himself so seriously; it was something appalling. Under all his culture, his cleverness, his amenity, under his good nature, his facility, his knowledge of life, his egotism lay hidden like a serpent in a bank of flowers. (II, 196)

(The characteristic fusion of the Gothic image and the disclaimer of actual violence—"Of course it had not been physical suffering"—exploits the affective power of terror, preserves it from the banality of melodrama, and prevents it from being dissipated or resolved through physical suffering, death, or overt violence.)

While recognizing that Isabel's meditations in this chapter bring her closer to self-awareness, particularly of those elements in her character that have made her vulnerable to Osmond, the reader perceives that the rhetorical emphasis in the chapter is placed squarely on the figure of Isabel as victim. Her suffering is proportional not to her errors, her naivete or egotism, but rather to her former desire to be free and extraordinary:

> It was a strange opposition, of the like of which she had never dreamed —an opposition in which the vital principle of the one was a thing of contempt to the other. It was not her fault—she had practiced no deception; she had only admired and believed. She had taken all the first steps in the purest confidence, and then she had suddenly found the infinite vista of a multiplied life to be a dark, narrow alley with a dead wall at the end. Instead of leading to the high places of happiness, from which the world would seem to lie below one, so that one could look down with a sense of exaltation and advantage, and judge and choose and pity, it led rather downward and earthward, into realms of restriction and depression where the sound of other lives, easier and freer, was heard as from above, and where it served to deepen the feeling of failure. (II, 189)

From this point in the action, James heightens our sense of Isabel's misery, and with equal skill, attempts to eliminate the possible solution to her problem: divorce or at least separation from her husband. Her friends, Warburton, Ralph, Henrietta, return to observe her marriage, to pity her, and with varying degrees of insight, to penetrate to the truth of that relation. Osmond's disappointment over losing Warburton brings his spite and his hatred for his wife into the open in the scene which begins Chapter Fifty-one. The chapter concludes with the Countess' revelations concerning the past relation between Osmond and Madame Merle. Isabel goes to England where Ralph is dying and there confronts her aunt with the information that Madame Merle has made a convenience out of her.

Isabel's humiliation is probed in various ways in these scenes, but each time in a manner which retains for her dignity and self-possession. Either she refuses to admit the truth about her marriage or she simply acknowledges it with great calm. Here, as frequently in James's work, the effort to conceal or minimize a grief for which the principal is not fully responsible is invested with a moral and aesthetic value seemingly unattainable by the effort, much more problematic, to eliminate the cause of that grief.

The scene at Ralph's deathbed brings together the whole second half of the novel as surely as Isabel's confrontations with her friends in Chapters Thirty-four and Thirty-five represent the structural climax of the first half. The scene focuses and intensifies the design of the novel, the polarities of freedom and submission. It makes the strongest possible appeal to the sympathy and admiration which Isabel's characterization has been designed to elicit. It so dignifies Isabel's acceptance of suffering through consciousness, that Goodwood's subsequent appeal is made to seem, by contrast, a passionate evasion, finally as irrelevant as the warnings of Isabel's friends to attend to common sense and the way of the world in choosing a husband.

Isabel has been punished, and severely so, but in agreeing to face and to accept the terms of her misfortune, so out of proportion to what she has deserved, she performs an act of will which is for James extraordinary and beautiful, much more so than anything Ralph had anticipated. For James, this acceptance is comparable to the magnificence of her desire to be free, a fact emphasized structurally by the comparable functions of Chapters Thirty-four and Thirty-five, and the scene at Ralph's bedside. The decision to accept, consciously, the terms of her suffering, like Isabel's desire to be free, is not primarily dictated by specific moral or psychological concerns. Rather it follows from James's initial conception of two splendidly evocative conditions, passionate freedom and humiliating submission, conditions absolute and uncompromised, incorporated in the history of a young woman interesting enough, by virtue of these polarities, to be by herself the center of our interest, the Jamesian heroine.

If we have been moved by Isabel's story, we may entertain the thought at the end of the novel that she will somehow extricate herself from her marriage. "Look here, Mr. Goodwood," says Henrietta, "just you wait," and projecting the Isabel we have observed into the aftermath of the novel, we encourage ourselves "to wait," despite the nagging sense that here, as elsewhere, Henrietta is being sensible and wrong. In his own comments on the ending of the novel James supplies arguing points both for those readers who look forward to Isabel's separation from Osmond and for those who deny the possibility of such an outcome.

> The obvious criticism of course will be that it is not finished—that I have not seen the heroine to the end of her situation—that I have left her *en l'air*. —— This is both true and false. The *whole* of anything is never told; you can only take what groups together . . . It is complete in itself—and the rest may be taken up or not, later.[13]

13. *Ibid.,* p. 18.

I myself believe that such hopes as those entertained by Henrietta are illusory, a kind of tribute to an only partly understood Isabel Archer. In our analysis we have traced the sequence of action by which Isabel rejects Warburton and Goodwood and chooses Osmond. The pattern observable here is not primarily that of consistent psychological development, although there are hints and pretexts enough to supply us indefinitely for controversy about Isabel's motivation. Rather, the relevant pattern, what I have called the design of the novel, is supplied by James's interest in a series of increasingly audacious acts of freedom, culminating in the heroine's decision to enslave herself. Similarly, the depiction of Isabel's marriage in the second half of the novel is not a working out of the moral consequences of naiveté, pride, imprudence, or sexual coldness. It is rather an evocation of misery proportional to the desire for freedom which Isabel embodies in the first half.

Isabel exists within and serves this design of radical polarity. In speculating about possible separation or divorce from Osmond, we ought to ask if such an outcome is compatible with James's own sense of, and fascination with this design. I think that it is not, and I think that James goes to some lengths to demonstrate this. For example, adultery was a conventional means of extricating one's heroine from a disastrous marriage, but Goodwood's appeal, though it affects Isabel strongly, is rejected. It is rejected by James because for him such an appeal, by Goodwood or future Goodwoods, threatened not so much the sanctity of marriage as the distinction of what his heroine has achieved through suffering a miserable one. Sexual passion, with the claim for freedom given it by Goodwood, is in direct competition with the Jamesian ideal of freedom won through suffering the consequences of intense illusions.

Both the illusions and Isabel's consequent suffering are made to seem heroic insofar as she undertakes to experience them alone, unaided by the support of friends or by what we might call the collective authority of social forms. The essence of Isabel's illusory hope for freedom has been the explicit rejection of social formulas which assert that the best that she can hope for in life is marriage, specifically marriage to a successful American businessman or a civilized English lord. I should say that the essence of Isabel's suffering, as prescribed by the author's conception of her, would be an equally positive rejection of the social forms available for relief from a bad marriage. Let us recall that these forms are given quite extensive treatment in James's accounts of the Countess Gemini, Madame Merle, and Mrs. Touchett. I am aware that the specifics of Isabel's character make it unlikely that she would emulate any of these three women in their manner of withdrawing from an unhappy marriage. But beyond this, the design in which James casts his heroine, which for him makes her heroic, stands in remarkable contrast to alternatives proposed by society and represented by these three women. These alternatives necessarily entail compromise, inconsistency, and evasion of the kind which, although commonplace in society, are simply incompatible with the Jamesian notion of the heroic, or with his fascination for radical, polarized opposition. Isabel will remain in her marriage to Osmond through the force of a personal will which, although sobered by knowledge, has lost none of its power to affront what society prescribes or what Henrietta regards as plain common sense.

This suggests that the experience which James regards as heroic, which he wished to celebrate in the person and in the career of his "free spirit," does not so much emerge out of, as it stands in contrast to the interplay of manners and morals that is social experience. The working out of the Jamesian design takes precedence over the depiction of social reality, just as it occasionally makes irrelevant the demand for strict psychological consistency. This last is the thesis we shall test in an analysis of *The Princess Casamassima.*

3

THE PRINCESS CASAMASSIMA

Hyacinth Robinson is taken by Miss Pynsent, a seamstress who cares for the boy, to visit his mother before she dies in prison. She has been confined there for murdering her lover. Later, as a young man, Hyacinth discovers that the lover, Sir Frederick Purvis, was his father. Raised by Miss Pynsent with an obscure sense of his own distinction, Hyacinth is trained as a bookbinder. He is loved and protected from some of the harshness of lower class London by Mr. Vetch, a musician reduced to playing in the music halls, and by the Poupins, an expatriate French couple who live through their English exile with the memory and the rhetoric of the barricades of 1871. Through the Poupins, Hyacinth meets Paul Muniment, a more determined, purposeful, and contemporary version of the revolutionary, who in turn passes him on to an interview with the mysterious anarchist, Dietrich Hoffendahl, before whom Hyacinth pledges to assassinate an influential reactionary should the cause of revolution require it. The young man makes such a pledge to prove the sincerity of his hatred for injustice and the misery of the London slums, a misery which he has directly experienced.

Hyacinth fails to keep his pledge. His hatred for the rich and

49

powerful has been from the first weakened by a capacity to appreciate what they enjoy. While his acquaintance with revolutionaries brings him closer to the violence by which he could express his hatred of the social order, a simultaneous series of encounters offers Hyacinth the chance to enjoy the art and leisure which, he is certain, that social order, although corrupt, nevertheless preserves. He meets the Princess Casamassima, spends a fortnight at an English country home, and wanders through Italy and France. He ends by hating the "beastly cause" to which he had pledged himself and loving that civilization which he earlier was fully content to see destroyed. The order comes from Hoffendahl to assassinate a duke. Hyacinth vaguely seeks aid from two women and a man in whom he had placed his trust. All three fail him, significantly because all are involved in sexual relations which prevent them from giving Hyacinth the parental love he seeks. The young man shoots himself.

There are two related designs figured in the action of *The Princess Casamassima*. The first, a radical conflict between alternating desires to destroy and to embrace the established order of society, James employed to control our understanding of, and reaction to Hyacinth Robinson. With the second design, which I shall examine later in this chapter, James drew a larger lesson than Hyacinth himself, limited by the terms of his experience, could be expected to articulate.

Hyacinth is marked throughout by his parentage, James exploiting a theme just then coming into prominence in the naturalistic novel, that of the transmission of instincts through heredity. But whereas characters such as Gervaise Macquart, and her daughter Nana, are shown by Zola to have inherited certain measured psychological dispositions which interact with environmental forces, Hyacinth Robinson falls heir to a complete identity. His life embodies the violent conflict imaged in his mother's murder of his father. Hyacinth is animated by alternate desires to destroy the social order over which his father helped to preside, and to enjoy the aesthetic and cultural fruits of that order. Unable to resolve the conflict, he kills himself, mother and father reconciled by the son who re-enacts and suffers their violence. The force of heredity figured in *The Princess Casamassima* is, so far as the action of the novel is concerned, more decisive than it appears to be in Zola's work. The origins of James's use of this theme lie with legend and fairy tale rather than with the tradition of the naturalistic or social novel of Zola or Balzac.

James used the design initially figured in Hyacinth's parents to structure his hero's relations with the other characters in the novel.[1] That is, the other characters stand in relation to Hyacinth in one or more of the roles suggested by the figures of his real parents, Florentine Vivier and Lord Frederick: a minor character may act as a parent who fosters one or the other of Hyacinth's polar impulses toward society; he may personally incorporate a contradiction similar to Hyacinth's own, and thus throw back reflected light upon the hero; he may abdicate as parent by submitting to passion (whether murderous hate, as in his real mother, or sex, as in her surrogates) and betray and abandon "poor Hyacinth."

A brief examination of these characters in their relations with Hyacinth indicates just how pervasively James employed his design. My summary does not falsify the relationships of the novel by emphasizing their schematic arrangement. Paul Muniment, Millicent Henning, Schinkel, and the rest exhibit in their relations with Hyacinth a sufficient variety of personal and social traits to satisfy our demand for detail in portraiture. I wish only to show that these characters exist in the novel primarily to subserve James's initial interest in the design figured in his hero.

My analysis should demonstrate that James's commitment was, first of all, to the evocative power of his design and only then to a verisimilitude chiefly designed to allay the resistance of the reader to his rigidly patterned fiction. Later in this chapter we shall examine instances in which the operation of his design proved incompatible with the demands of strict verisimilitude. For the moment, in stressing the pattern which underlies the variety of detail, I wish to isolate the essential function of the novel's subordinate characters, a function which I believe to have been dictated by James's conception of a character, a fictional young man, rather than by the impact upon his consciousness of the inhabitants of a real city.

Miss Pynsent and Mr. Vetch are the first pair of foster parents provided Hyacinth in the novel. Miss Pynsent, whose notions of society are clipped from the *London Illustrated News,* and framed by reverence for the genteel, encourages Hyacinth to regard himself as dis-

1. Ward, in *The Search for Form,* p. 128, mentions the moral and structural significance of Hyacinth's relations with his surrogate parents. But he is more concerned with other recurrent elements in the novel: "the artistic and quasi-artistic activities of many of the characters, their theatricalism, the allusions to Dickens—explicit and implicit—and other nineteenth-century novelists, . . . the emphasis on light and darkness in general, the pastoral scenes standing in sharp contrast to the dominant urban drabness." These elements, he argues, are more significant than Hyacinth's relations with his surrogate parents, for they help to define the structure of London society, and for Ward (p. 116) "the subject of *The Princess* is London."

tinguished by his noble blood, although she can barely bring herself to contemplate, much less speak of, the manner in which that blood was transmitted. From the time of his earliest youth, Pynnie interposes herself between Hyacinth and the influences of lower class London. She ensures that in manner, dress, and gesture, he will be a gentleman, helping to create out of her illusions a copy more engaging, if less equipped for survival, than the original. When she dies, it is Miss Pynsent's money which Hyacinth uses to go to France, where his desire for beauty is for once satisfied.

Mr. Vetch is a reformer of mild and skeptical cast, who admires Hyacinth's spirit without indulging so heartily as Miss Pynsent in phantasies about his birth. But he also loves and tries to protect Hyacinth. He contributes to the small inheritance which sends the young man to Paris, and the fulfillment of one half of James's design. Upon Hyacinth's return, Mr. Vetch is astute enough to realize that he is entangled in a violent political scheme, and goes to the Princess to plead in effect for his foster son's life. In this he fails, in fact, is totally ineffectual in a scene which, interestingly enough, W. J. Harvey has singled out as affronting the reader's sense of probability, given what we know of Mr. Vetch.[2] But James has been true to *his* conception of Vetch, determined by the author's notion of his relation to Hyacinth: he is one of the several fathers in the novel who, for all of their love for Hyacinth, prove finally unable to save him.

That Eustache Poupin and his wife are also to be seen as surrogate parents who fail Hyacinth is clearly indicated at a number of points in the text. Poupin finds the young man a job, trains him as a bookbinder, and brings him around to his flat to be mothered by Madame Poupin and inspired with tales of the Commune. Here Hyacinth first meets Paul Muniment. James regards the couple as harmless in their rhetoric, gentle in their love for Hyacinth, and pathetically, absurdly caught in a conflict between the two when the summons from Hoffendahl finally comes to a Hyacinth who has lost all his former political convictions. Nevertheless they fail him. As Pynnie and Mr. Vetch nourished in Hyacinth the sense of innate aristocracy which sends him toward disillusionment at the hands of the Princess, so does Poupin help to direct the young man's envy and frustration, the legacy from his mother, toward anarchism and his own death. The Frenchman ceases his efforts to prevent Hyacinth from adhering to his pledge when a remark of his leads Poupin to suppose, wrongly, that Hyacinth has regained ideological purity:

2. Harvey, *Character and the Novel,* pp. 86-87.

"Ah well, if you *are* with us that's all I want to know!" the young man heard [Poupin] call from the top of the stairs in a different voice, a tone of sudden extravagant fortitude.[3]

Captain Sholto and Millicent Henning are interesting amalgamations of the possible roles suggested by Hyacinth's parents, though they are rather less obviously placed in accordance with James's design. Still, Sholto bears a resemblance to Lord Frederick, and in a carefully developed scene early in the novel he is made to awaken Hyacinth's admiration by the ease of his manner and the casual refinement of his apartment. Millicent, as most critics point out, carries into the novel something of the energy and the shrewdness of lower class London, and her own sensual vitality. But in his treatment of her relation with Hyacinth, James stresses the maternal quality of her affection, which is clearly what Hyacinth seeks:

> She was crude, she was common, she even had the vice of pointless exaggeration, for he himself honestly couldn't understand how the situation he had described could make him nicer. But when the faculty of affection that was in her rose to the surface it diffused a glow of rest, almost of protection. . . . It seemed a pause in something harsh that was happening to him, making it all easier, pushing it off to a distance. (II, 340)

The rest, the protection, and the comfort of Millicent's affection are finally denied him when Hyacinth is most in need of them, as he wanders in search of some escape from his pledge to Hoffendahl. Entering the store where Millicent works, he finds her posed before Captain Sholto, "his eyes traveling up and down the front of their beautiful friend's person." (II, 423) Hyacinth turns and leaves the store without speaking. Critics regularly treat this scene as one of a succession of betrayals by which the hero's friends finally abandon him to suicide. But, it is easy to misread the type of betrayal which James intends. For example, Hyacinth does not here lose the woman whom he himself desires, for James is careful to avoid suggestion of this in his treatment of the relationship. The young man loses Millicent, not sexually, but to sex, that passion seen here, as so often in James, as inimical to the sympathy required by his major character. Also, sexual passion in Millicent is here implicitly associated with the violent passion which, in Florentine Vivier, originally deprived Hyacinth of maternal love and protection.

Each of the characters discussed above, besides standing in relation to Hyacinth in the role of foster parent, also personally incorpor-

3. James, *The Princess,* II, p. 372.

ates a form of the contradiction by which Hyacinth's identity is shaped. In each case the contradiction is less extravagant than it appears in Hyacinth Robinson, a fact which tends to diminish our sense of the fabulous in the hero's origins. Less extreme contradictions of the same type, manifest in each of these characters and expressed in socially recognizable and credible terms, lend to Hyacinth a verisimilitude which, in isolation in the novel, he would not have. But, once again, what is essential is that the minor contradictions stressed in the subordinate characters are in the novel chiefly because they point up the polarities of Hyacinth Robinson; Hyacinth in return borrows from such characters as Millicent Henning and Pynnie a credibility which allows the evocative power of James's design to operate freely.

Miss Pynsent lives in near poverty and at the same time exhibits a wholly unqualified admiration for "society," rather like the feelings expressed so torturously by the heroine of "In the Cage." Vetch has more, not less integrity as an artist and a gentleman because he plays in a music hall and lives in a cheap room. The Poupins, on the other hand, reflect in comic vein, the curious mixture of bourgeois respectability and bloody rhetoric which Hyacinth himself shows us at the end of the first volume of the novel. Captain Sholto is a social aristocrat who dabbles in revolution for the sake of being able to bring new "specimens" to the Princess. Hyacinth admires his urbanity, dislikes him personally, and ends by assuming his office in service of the Princess, bringing her Paul Muniment, his own replacement. Millicent is the shopgirl who believes in the social order because she knows it is within her power to enter it, a cockney princess who does not merely dream of drawing rooms, but fully intends to enter and dominate them. Lady Aurora and Rose Muniment function hardly at all as agents in the plot. They exist, particularly Rose Muniment, as further illustrations of the type of contradiction figured in Hyacinth. Lady Aurora suffers agonies of quiet shame over her high position in society, but in the end settles back into it. Rose Muniment conducts a kind of working class salon from a sickbed, where she protests her love for wealth and power and jabs maliciously at the real and prospective aristocrats brought to her bedside.

These characters, by virtue of contradictions integral to their very existence in the novel, direct the reader's attention back toward Hyacinth and the polar design which he embodies. Once again, the usefulness of a schematic description such as the one that I have given above is that it enables the reader of the novel to see that the principle of invention by which these characters entered *The Princess*

Casamassima, although not incompatible with the author's direct observation of the London scene, is almost surely not confined to such observation. James's peculiar signature upon the characterization of *The Princess Casamassima* is not the variety nor concreteness of his portrayals, although these are genuine strengths, but rather the underlying aesthetic control exercised over them. In the end, this control makes each of the minor characters a product of Hyacinth's conflict, and only thereafter, a product of the London streets.

James fashioned the minor characters so that their first reference would be toward Hyacinth rather than outward toward social or economic facts about which James had only casual knowledge. Similarly, the action, the ordinary events of the novel, is devised so as to turn our attention toward aesthetic interests of which James is in full control, rather than types of experience which he knew chiefly from the newspaper. There are no strikes represented in the novel, no direct treatment of hunger or the physical discomfort or tediousness of ordinary labor. There is only one summarily detailed picture of Hyacinth at the bindery where he is employed. Both the crowd scene in The Sun and Moon Tavern, and the meetings which take place at the home of a working man, Paul Muniment, are very carefully translated into terms which James found easy to deal with. The workers who crowd The Sun and Moon during the winter, in which "forty thousand men are out of work in the east of London," are sluggish and aimless in their complaints, scorned by Muniment. By emphasizing the note of personal sluggishness, a mental torpor which, but for the vocabulary, James might as easily have found in a dinner party companion, he avoided the need to treat particular social origins of such stagnation. And what he shows us of Muniment and his sister in their home is not what must have been the ordinary course of life for a working man and his crippled sister in London of the 1880's. James avoids these aspects for the sake of such structurally convenient features as Rose Muniment's inveterate love of the English aristocracy, and Muniment's obliging habit of bringing home specimens from various social classes. The latter habit is implausible both in the light of current social realities and of what we know of Muniment. It, however, does provide James with a pretext for dramatizing paradoxical combinations of social types, the emphasis in such scenes being on the paradox of their meeting rather than on the substantive experience of those who meet.

The literal action of the novel is then largely confined to encounters among the characters, conversations, walks through the city streets,

Hyacinth's visit to Paris, much the sort of event James dealt with in all of his fiction, until the suicide which concludes the novel. Tranquil and unobtrusive though it may be, such action is very carefully shaped by James to augment the force of the design incorporated in Hyacinth. For example, he employs the technique of repetition, the duplication of the essential features of an earlier scene, for the sake both of advancing the action and of reinforcing our sense of the permanent elements in his plot. James makes perfectly clear what we are to regard as the most important permanent element of his plot, and with this in mind we quickly grasp the relevance of the repetitive pattern which emerges when we survey all the episodes which comprise the novel. Here, for example, is one of several descriptions of the force which animates Hyacinth.

> Sometimes, in imagination, he sacrificed one of the authors of his being to the other, throwing over Lord Frederick much the oftener; sometimes, when the theory failed that his father would have done great things for him if he had lived, or the assumption broke down that he had been Florentine Vivier's only lover, he cursed and disowned them alike; sometimes he arrived at conceptions which presented them side by side, looking at him with eyes infinitely sad but quite unashamed—eyes that seemed to tell him they had been surpassingly unfortunate but had not been base. Of course his worst moments now, as they had always been the worst, were those in which his grounds for holding that Lord Frederick had really been his father viciously fell away from him. It must be added that they always passed off, since the mixture in his tormenting, his incorrigible pulses could be accounted for by no other dream.
>
> I mention these dim broodings not because they belong in an especial degree to the history of our young man during the winter of the Princess's residence in Madeira Crescent, *but because they were a constant element in his moral life and need to be remembered in any view of him at a given time.* [italics mine] (II, 265-66)

This is a straightforward account of Hyacinth's state of mind upon returning from Paris. It is thus a psychological version of the design that is etched into every aspect of the novel, a design which, over and over again, the seemingly trivial lines of action are made to trace. Repeatedly Hyacinth begins to, or at least tries to sacrifice "one of the authors of his being to the other." Thus the small boy's shudder of revulsion when confronted with the miserable and strange woman who speaks French and wants to embrace him, the shudder of revulsion which draws him back into Pynnie's protective arms and the gentility which she represents. The passionate outburst in The Sun and Moon Tavern is, on the other hand, an equally impulsive movement *toward* his mother, an attempt to share in the rage which drove her. Thus, also the succession of appeals, the visits to Vetch, Poupin, Muniment, all of whom do something for him, but not enough, and who disappoint him at last, as his father had disappointed him even beyond his death through the utter neglect of Lord Frederick's family. And one way in which we can make sense of the jealousy which Hyacinth experiences as he observes both the Princess and Millicent with other men, is to refer back to the boy's doubts about his mother's fidelity to her aristocratic lover.

Other patterns emerge as well. When his real mother dies, it is certain that Pynnie will preside over the formation of those genteel elements of his character which, in James's scheme, he has inherited from his father. In a similar way, Pynnie's death and the inheritance she provides him allow the young man, for once and only briefly, to find something in Paris equal to his capacity for appreciation. Actions initiated by the Princess also tend to be repetitive enactments of one basic situation. She finds and takes up Hyacinth to gratify her desire for proximity to the working class. Such proximity will, she hopes, allow her to have a hand in the destruction of the sterile order of society which her husband personifies, and somehow ease the sexual desire which that same husband has been unable to satisfy. Hyacinth fails her, but Muniment does not. The point here is that the dramatically rendered manoeuvers of the Princess to effect this end are precisely similar with both men. The pattern, a discarded version of which we find in her relation with Sholto, asserts itself in substantially the same form with Hyacinth and Paul.

Besides using patterns of repetition, James structures the action of his novel by the simultaneous treatment of Hyacinth's dual but contradictory impulses toward society. In neatly measured steps he moves toward the impasse in which, by his return from Paris, he has managed to fix himself: formally pledged to destroy, but emotionally committed to a defense of society. To be sure, the contradiction is already imaged for us in the first long scene of the novel, the episode of Hyacinth's visit to the prison where he meets his mother. Pynnie's preparations for that trip underline the curiously fastidious, even rather ironic qualities of the boy's nature, so that we fully expect him to be as frightened and as shocked by the experience as he is. What James conveys in the scene, an idea which dominates the whole history of his sensitive youth, is that given the radical polarity imaged in the encounter between this twelve-year-old gentleman and the dying murderess, no compromise, no qualified but lasting satisfaction for Hyacinth Robinson, is going to be possible. And this is what sharply distinguishes the use which James makes of this episode from the use to which such episodes were typically put by Dickens, the writer whose technique James is thought to have drawn upon for the rendition of the scene. A similarity in descriptive and even dramatic techniques makes the comparison useful, it is true, but the function of such a scene in Dickens, in a novel like *Great Expectations,* for example, is to initiate substantial change, moral or social, usually both, in the protagonist. James intends precisely the opposite. Hyacinth, the young gentleman, encounters in his mother a truth which will make such Dickensian developments as change, adaptation, and compromise impossible. In Dickens, such a scene, through the shock of encounter, brings movement. In James, the long episode of Hyacinth's visit to prison is the dramatic announcement of an impasse which, because centered in the very identity of the hero, can never be broken, only temporarily evaded.

What appears then to be a progressive action is rather a working and reworking in dramatic form of the design which James has projected for his hero, an intensification of the terms of the impasse in which Hyacinth finds himself from the very first. What changes is the breadth and intensity of Hyacinth's understanding of his situation. And, as is the case with Milly Theale, Strether, and, to a lesser degree, Isabel Archer, what gives special pathos and intensity to the full consciousness of the hero is the imminence of death or disillusionment.

The action of the novel is a carefully gradated series of events and encounters designed to work out plausibly on the literal level of the story what is implicit in the tableau-like scene which James presents in the encounter between Hyacinth and his mother. The young man, in the first half of the novel, moves steadily from the influence of Mr. Vetch to that of Poupin, and through Muniment to the secret meeting with Dietrich Hoffendahl, and hence to an actualization of the tendency first figured in the person of his mother. Similarly, and simultaneously with the movement along political lines, Hyacinth starts off under the protection of Pynnie, thence to Millicent, who has fewer illusions about but no less respect for the established order. He next meets Lady Aurora who prefigures the Princess, and who begins to elicit from Hyacinth the admiration for charm, ease and wealth called forth in full tide by the Princess Casamassima. The order of carefully gradated ascent is perfect, and its structural climax comes in the long scene at the country house at Medley which James uses as a frame for Hyacinth's account of the meeting with Hoffendahl.

The existence of such a neatly symmetrical pattern of action in the first half of the novel reveals several important things about the kind of book that James was writing. We may admit first of all that, as in his characterization of the minor figures of the novel, there is nothing in the action which I have summarized, no single event, which strikes us as resoundingly false to our knowledge of lower class London of the eighties. The workers did meet in one another's homes for political discussion, wrangle over ideologies and methods, and walk the streets together on Sundays, since this was the only time and form of leisure they could afford. The skilled workers, such as those in the trade which Hyacinth follows, were generally the most militant, and no doubt were much more likely to meet representatives of the various radical groups than a miner or day laborer.[4] So no single encounter of Hyacinth's in this first half of the novel is beyond belief.

But the simultaneous arrangement of the two series of encounters by which Hyacinth involves himself with the revolutionary and the aristocratic world, the *form* in which James puts his material together here, has a logic and a purpose quite distinct from that of mimetic, representational fiction. Negatively, the schematic arrangement of the action operates as an aesthetic control against the diffusiveness that any serious or sustained treatment of social, political, or economic themes would necessarily involve. The logic of repetition, ascending orders of involvement, and simultaneity fasten our attention upon Hyacinth and make the pattern of his adventures much closer to the form of allegory than to mimetic fiction, in which, necessarily, the action partakes of something of the variety and disproportion exhibited in the hero's social or moral milieu. The very tightness of James's form, considered rhetorically, prevents us from pausing for a thorough consideration of the moral or social significance of Hyacinth's encounters, *either* with the exponents of the established order or with the "revolutionaries." With such minor figures as Miss Pynsent and Eustache Poupin, James uses comedy to dissuade us from taking their opinions or their lives very seriously as representative of a social or political ethic. As a matter of fact, insofar as they consciously insist

4. Howe, *Politics,* p. 145. But about the accuracy with which James described the political structures and activities of revolutionaries in England there is considerable controversy. Trilling, *The Liberal Imagination,* p. 68, maintains that "there is not a political event of *The Princess Casamassima,* not a detail of oath or mystery or danger, which is not confirmed by multitudinous records." On the other hand, Woodcock, "Henry James and the Conspirators," p. 228, argues that "there is no important detail in which the Jamesian conspirators can be identified with the historical Anarchists, who have remained to this day a loose collection of individuals and groups devoted to spontaneous direct action and personal propaganda rather than conspiracy."

on a correspondence between *their* experience and a principle, be it British decorum or French *égalité,* capable of governing the larger social order, they become, and are shown to be, comic characters. Here, as often in his work, James uses comedy to deflate the claims of abstract ideas, uncongenial to him not as a moralist but as the artist of a type of intense individualism which frequently demanded abstract passion but foundered on abstract ideas.

Even at the most important points in the action, for example, the first meetings with Muniment and the Princess, James discourages us from a careful consideration of social issues. One simple way he does this is by making the conversations, of which, after all, the book is largely made up, impenetrably vague whenever political ideas are at stake. The quotation that follows is a lengthy one but necessary to catch the tone and the rhythm of a conversation that in some such form is repeated over and over again in the novel. Rose Muniment is describing Lady Aurora:

> She was so ashamed of being rich that she wondered the lower classes didn't break into Inglefield and take possession of all the treasures in the Italian room. She was a tremendous socialist; she was worse than anyone—she was worse even than Paul.
> "I wonder if she's worse than me," Hyacinth returned at a venture, . . .
> "Hullo, I didn't know you were so advanced!" exclaimed [Paul], who had been sitting silent and sidewise in a chair that was too narrow for him, his big arm hugging the back. "Have we been entertaining an angel unawares?"
> Hyacinth made out he was chaffing him, but he knew the way to face that sort of thing was to exaggerate one's meaning. "You didn't know I was advanced? Why, I thought that was the principal thing about me. I think I go about as far as any one."
> "I thought the principal thing about you was that you knew French," Paul Muniment said with an air of derision which showed him he wouldn't put that ridicule upon him unless he liked him, at the same time that it revealed to him how he had come within an ace of posturing.
> "Well, I don't know it for nothing. I'll say something that will take your head off if you don't look out—just the sort of thing they say so well in French."
> "Oh, do say something of that kind; we should enjoy it so much!" cried Rosy in perfect good faith and clasping her hands for expectation.
> The appeal was embarrassing, but Hyacinth was saved from the consequences of it by a remark from Lady Aurora, who quavered out the words after two or three false starts, appearing to address him, now that she spoke to him directly, with a sort of overdone consideration. "I should like so very much to know—it would be so interesting—if you don't mind—how far exactly you do go." She threw back her head very far and thrust her shoulders forward, and if her chin had been more adapted to such a purpose would have appeared to point it at him.

This challenge was hardly less alarming than the other, for he was far from being ready with an impressive formula. He replied, however, with a candour in which he tried as far as possible to sink his vagueness: "Well, I'm very strong indeed. I think I see my way to conclusions from which even Monsieur and Madame Poupin would shrink. Poupin, at any rate; I'm not so sure about his wife."

"I should like so much to know Madame," Lady Aurora murmured as if politeness demanded that she should content herself with this answer.

"Oh, Poupin isn't strong," said Muniment; "you can easily look over his head! He has a sweet assortment of phrases—they're really pretty things to hear, some of them; but he hasn't had a new idea these thirty years. It's the old stock that has been withering in the window. All the same he warms one up; he has a spark of the sacred fire." (I, 128-31)

What is at stake here, and in all such conversations in the novel, is not an attempt to depict through the experience of characters the interplay of social forces which, when we are abstracting, we call Christian socialism, anarchism, or whatever; rather James presents us with a number of people who wish most desperately to validate their experience by proving that they do, indeed, "go far," or "take a certain line." I don't want to overlook the quite intentional element of humor in the excerpt I have just quoted, particularly that achieved by using Rosy as half-malicious counterpoint, and by playing the anxieties of Hyacinth and Lady Aurora off against the perfect self-confidence of Muniment. But the essential feature of the talk in this scene, as in speeches by the Princess in which the ironic note is more muted, is vague reference *infused with* the passionate desire to "go far."

What James does by ushering Hyacinth Robinson through encounters such as these, and the complementary series of encounters with Sholto, Millicent, and the Princess, is to ensure that, so far as the literal terms of the story are concerned, Hyacinth will "go far." That is, that he will arrive at intimacy with a real princess and a German anarchist, and through this intimacy provide the reader with a concrete expression of the conflicting desires which both animate and frustrate him. The action then is not the means by which James renders for us the interplay of social and political forces in London of the eighties, but rather the pretext for an increasingly intense revelation of the conflict, almost geometrical in its polarity, which exists within Hyacinth Robinson and indeed explains his very existence in the novel.

There were times when he said to himself that it might very well be his fate to be divided to the point of torture, to be split open by sympathies that pulled him in different ways; for hadn't he an extraordinarily mingled current in his blood, and from the time he could remember wasn't there one half of him always either playing tricks on the other or getting snubs and pinches from it? (I, 171)

Hyacinth does "go far" in the novel by the series of encounters which James arranges for him. For all of his emotion, he is sufficiently passive to be moved by his creator very quickly up to the twin summits of anarchism and the grand life of Medley. He is made to go far through an action which, while assuring that the reader will register a princess and a practicing anarchist as, in their respective directions, pretty far indeed, also strictly prevents us from excursions into either the concrete terms or the broader social implications of what is believed in so passionately. What matters for James is Hyacinth's polar and ultimately self-destructive passions. What matters rhetorically is that we register, in our reading, the intensity of this passion. Since neither Hyacinth's dilemma nor our reaction to it can exist in the total absence of fact and event, James gives us an action. That action makes use of just enough plausible detail to exhibit and bring to a state of high tension what Yvor Winters has called an intense situation,[5] and to evoke from the reader the sympathy for Hyacinth which James intends. What I take to be James's rhetorical purpose in this first half of the novel dictates the following strategy. Realistic details and political ideas, while they have a certain representational value in themselves, operate mainly to distract us from the design incorporated personally in Hyacinth and exhibited by the action. The design is the polar conflict between the desire to destroy and the desire to defend and cherish. His sense of ordinary reality soothed by the presence of concrete details, the reader is willing to submit to the considerable evocative power which James can generate from polarized conflict.

By taking the first half of the novel apart in this fashion, I have short-circuited the effect that James intended and made the form of the action seem a good deal more artificial than it actually appears on a normally attentive reading of the book. This I have done in order to point up the crucial importance in James's work of the link between a symmetrically patterned action or situation and an emotional intensity which is both rhetorically effective and largely inexplicable when one tries to account for it in the specific social and moral issues rendered. The action persuades us to take Hyacinth seriously, not finally as a "young man from the provinces," or a little bookbinder caught up in social and political forces he does not fully understand. We take him seriously as the locus of a polar conflict exhibited in

5. Winters, *Defense of Reason*, p. 320.

such a way as to elicit our interest and sympathy. Specifically, we are to feel sympathy for one who is trapped, a victim by birth, an unwitting but enthusiastic accomplice in a defeat which is only a more intense version of the impasse in which Robinson has struggled from the very first.

This I believe was the effect which James wished to achieve in the novel as a whole. Although it seems to me that at a few points in the first half James lays more stress on Hyacinth's passivity than our sympathy will bear, he nevertheless succeeds reasonably well in this section. However subject to the influence of others Hyacinth may be, however quick to yield to the glamour of aristocracy or revolution, the young man does act and he appears to want to assume responsibility for his actions, even when he does not wholly control them. It is thus possible to concede to James, in our response to his hero, something of the pathos, if not yet the tragedy of Hyacinth's dilemma.

The major problem in the novel begins in Book Four. This begins with the scene in which Hyacinth sits in a cafe in Paris and reflects on the qualitative change in his experience which the trip to Europe has brought about. In one sense it is the most successful, that is, the most moving and intense rendering of Hyacinth's situation. He is now fully conscious of what he has to lose when he receives the summons from Hoffendahl. And yet, this is also the point at which the novel, considered as both a coherent and an evocative treatment of the design of polar conflict, begins to deteriorate.

The reasons for this falling off I can best analyze by turning to two key passages in the Preface to the novel, in which James described his initial conception of Hyacinth and what he wished to make of him. He imagined the young man as seeing in London what Henry James had seen, feeling something of the American's own fascination with the life of the city. However, Hyacinth Robinson was to have been at first barred from the drawing rooms which the author had found open to him:

> I arrived so at the history of little Hyacinth Robinson—he sprang up for me out of the London pavement. To find his possible adventure interesting I had only to conceive his watching the same public show, the same innumerable appearances, I had watched myself, and of his watching very much as I had watched; save indeed for one little difference. This difference would be that so far as all the swarming facts should speak of freedom and ease, knowledge and power, money, opportunity and satiety, he should be able to revolve round them but at the most respectful of distances and with every door of approach shut in his face. For one's self, all conveniently, there had been doors that

opened—opened into light and warmth and cheer, into good and charming relations; and if the place as a whole lay heavy on one's consciousness there was yet always for relief this implication of one's own lucky share of the freedom and ease, lucky acquaintance with the number of lurking springs at light pressure of which particular vistas would begin to recede, great lighted, furnished, peopled galleries, sending forth gusts of agreeable sound.[6]

What is most notable about James's conception of his young man is that his plight consists not in his lack of power, wealth, or knowledge, but in his being prevented from the close observation of what other men have created out of these. From the first he is distinguished by his capacity to appreciate, and yet he is denied access to that class of society whose function it is to serve as a kind of repository for the accumulated artistic and cultural wealth of a nation. Hyacinth wants to examine these riches directly, at first hand; but there is no indication by the author, either in text or Preface, that his hero wants to take or create for himself. This makes Hyacinth different from the legendary "young man from the provinces" in whose tradition Lionel Trilling has placed this novel.[7] Julien Sorel wants to take; his is the story, initially at least, of frustrated desire. Hyacinth, as clearly projected in the mind of his creator, wants to observe; his is the story of frustrated sensibility.

But what would be the effect of . . . having so many precious things perpetually in one's eyes, yet of missing them all for any closer knowledge, and of the confinement of closer knowledge entirely to matters with which a connexion, however intimate, couldn't possibly pass for a privilege?[8]

In James's mind this kind of frustration was sufficiently strong to generate in Hyacinth an envy and a bitterness that would turn him toward "an aggressive, vindictive, destructive social faith," with its "treasons, stratagems, and spoils."[9] But once he is freed from frustration, once his sensibility is released and his consciousness stimulated by two weeks at a grand English country home or a few months in Europe, Hyacinth is purged of his envy and hatred.

In a letter to the Princess from Venice he expresses the change that has taken place in him, a change which, we have seen, is actually a final assertion of the delicate sensibility present in him from the first, but always before curbed.

6. *Art of the Novel*, pp. 60-1.
7. Trilling, *The Liberal Imagination*, pp. 61-5.
8. *The Art of the Novel*, p. 61.
9. *Ibid.*, p. 72.

The monuments and treasures of art, the great palaces and properties, the conquests of learning and taste, the general fabric of civilisation as we know it, based if you will upon all the despotisms, the cruelties, the exclusions, the monopolies and the rapacities of the past, but thanks to which, all the same, the world is less of a 'bloody sell' and life more of a lark—our friend Hoffendahl seems to me to hold them too cheap and to wish to substitute for them something in which I can't somehow believe as I do in things with which the yearnings and the tears of generations have been mixed. You know how extraordinary I think our Hoffendahl—to speak only of him; but if there's one thing that's more clear about him than another, it's that he wouldn't have the least feeling for this incomparable abominable old Venice. He would cut up the ceilings of the Veronese into strips, so that everyone might have a little piece. (II, 145-46)

Once given the chance to observe the Veronese, Hyacinth renounces the cause of Hoffendahl, who would cut it up into little pieces. But clearly what James wants us to recognize is that Hoffendahl's course of action, whatever decision he might make about the Veronese, would destroy the rich consciousness that has finally emerged in Hyacinth through his trip to Europe. Hoffendahl would destroy in men that almost mystic power which James celebrated in all of his books and felt in himself, the power to passionately observe and respond to the diverse stimuli of tradition, art, and social relations. The revolutionary threatens this passionate observer, and no amount of redistribution of bread, land, or power could outweigh this threat for James. Revolutionaries offer action and justice, but only at the cost of a human power which James used the whole range of his technique to celebrate: the power to experience intensely the richness, beauty, or complexity of some segment of one's individual experience. This power, reaching its heights in such characters as Lambert Strether and Milly Theale, may be couched in moral or social terms. But actually, as a careful study of the texts reveals, this power, by all the craft and strength of James's art, is made to transcend both the moral and the social orders. It is religious in its intensity and in the value which James accorded it. Hyacinth became an anarchist because he had the capacity but not the opportunity to exercise this power. He renounces anarchism when the opportunity becomes available.

What becomes increasingly apparent in the novel, from the scene in Paris to the conclusion, is that the whole social and political content of the novel, as well as the theme of hereditary determinism, is exploited to dramatize the plight of the frustrated observer. The design which we first examined, the conflict between polarized elements in Hyacinth Robinson, is a part of a larger conception taking the form

of a conflict between social and political power, *however exercised,*
and the individual's capacity to be, as James put it in his Preface,
"finely aware and richly responsible."[10] I think that Irving Howe,
whose study of *The Princess Casamassima* is one of the most acute,
misses this central point about the novel when he says that James
"had no larger view of politics as a collective mode of action."[11] In fact
the novel reveals that although James's knowledge of specifics may
have been dim, he had grasped both the elements of collectivity and
of action that are involved in politics, and he saw both as threats to
"consciousness." In this sense I would call the novel deeply anti-
political.

If I am right, then James could not conclude his novel with Book
Four, the point where Hyacinth, while pledged to murder and resigned
to his own death, has experienced most deeply a new consciousness of
life. Beyond deciding that Hyacinth must stick to his vow—for to let
him off on the grounds that he no longer believes would be for James,
we now clearly recognize, to diminish the intensity of both past and
present conviction—James cannot allow the message to come immediately from Hoffendahl. He cannot do this in spite of the fact that it
would seem dramatically and rhetorically logical that the long awaited
message should come just when Hyacinth has most to lose. For to
do so would limit the tragedy to Hyacinth and the meaning of
the novel to the design figured in him personally. What James
attempts in the two books which remain is to make of Hyacinth
the emblem of the Jamesian consciousness, and to try to demonstrate
the superiority of this power when judged against the pretensions of a
collective morality and political action. In Hyacinth's case, as with
many of James's heroes of his middle period, the final act of celebration is victimization, and so in this last section of the novel, James
undertakes at considerable lengths the betrayal of Hyacinth and the
consciousness he now represents.

This is managed through the characterization of Paul Muniment
and the Princess in the last third of the novel. It is not to James's
purpose to concentrate on personal villainy in these two, although in
the coldness of the former, and the passion of the latter, as these
affect Hyacinth, they bear a resemblance to Osmond and Madame
Merle. Rather, James focuses on elements in their characters which
he shrewdly recognized would be less striking as personal faults than
as symptoms of the evils to which political thought and action are

10. *Ibid.,* p. 62.
11. Howe, *Politics,* p. 150.

liable. Muniment—and the note is struck whenever he appears—is intense and narrow in his commitment to political action. He is finally willing to subordinate every feeling, including affection for Hyacinth and sexual desire for the Princess, to expediency as defined by his political ideals. On the other hand, James portrays through the Princess Casamassima the type of restless self-indulgence and deflected energy, in her case sexual, which sometimes underlies political acts or beliefs.

Even on the very rare occasions in the novel when Paul Muniment is allowed to articulate the political ideals he holds, James contrives, by contrasting them with simple but strong feeling in Hyacinth, to deflate their force. Thus, when the two men take a holiday after Hyacinth's return, the latter accuses Paul of wanting "for all mankind . . . the selfsame shade of asininity." Paul turns back the thrust skillfully:

> "That's very neat; did you pick it up in France? Damn the too-neat, you know; it's as bad as the too-rotten. The low tone of our fellow mortals is a result of bad conditions; it's the conditions I want to alter. When those who have no start to speak of have a good one it's but fair to infer they'll go further. I want to try them, you know." (II, 216)

But, lest this prove too strong a statement in favor of collective political action, James redresses the balance in the paragraph which ends the chapter:

> There was a strain of heroism in [Hyacinth's] words—of heroism of which the sense was not conveyed to Muniment by a vibration in their interlocked arms. Hyacinth didn't make the reflexion that he was infernally literal; he dismissed the sentimental problem that had worried him; he condoned, excused, admired—he merged himself, resting happy for the time, in the consciousness that Paul was a grand person, that friendship was a purer feeling than love and that there was an immense deal of affection between them. He didn't even observe at that moment that it was preponderantly on his own side. (II, 219)

The "sentimental problem" referred to in this passage is Hyacinth's bewilderment that Paul could contemplate his probable death with such equanimity. Clearly, this coldness of Muniment's is to be taken not just as a personal failing but also as a quality inherent in any generalized theory or collective action. Note the manner in which James, using Hyacinth's innocence as a foil, turns his irony from Muniment to that which Muniment is made to represent in the conflict between an intense personal consciousness and political action:

> Muniment's absence of passion, his fresh-coloured coolness, his easy exact knowledge, the way he kept himself clean (save for fine chemical

stains on his hands) in circumstances of foul contact, constituted a group
of qualities that had always appeared to [Hyacinth] singularly enviable.
Most enviable of all was the force that enabled him to sink personal
sentiment *where a great public good was to be attempted* [italics mine]
and yet keep up the form of caring for that minor interest. It seemed
to our young friend that if *he* had introduced a young fellow to Hoffendahl for his purposes, and Hoffendahl had accepted him on such a
recommendation and everything had been settled, he would have pre-
ferred never to look at the young fellow again. (II, 137-38)

This last sentence reveals the difficulty into which James fell with
his decision to expand the novel beyond the design of contradictory
impulses figured in Hyacinth. The evocative force of that design
depends on our perceiving that Hyacinth pledged his life to the
anarchists as a powerful, if not wholly self-conscious gesture of bitterness, rage over having been denied the full exercise of a human power.
The violence of the gesture is used by the author to enhance in the
mind of the reader the value of the experience denied the hero. But,
whereas we can be moved by the fate of one whose deprivation is so
severe as to lead him toward virtual self-destruction, we find it much
harder to respond to Hyacinth as "a young fellow" *introduced* by
Muniment to Hoffendahl "for his purposes." This is the Hyacinth of
the last third of the novel, who, if not actually led astray by Muniment,
has at least been callously abandoned by the radical leader.

In short, Hyacinth the victim, innocent, affectionate, mildly
reproachful, staunchly determined not to release himself from a now
meaningless vow—this is not a character of tragic self-contradiction,
but rather the emblematic Jamesian observer betrayed by ideology
and narrow morality. As James lays more and more stress on the
betrayal of Hyacinth, he undercuts the basis of our former respect.
After all, we were earlier persuaded that he was ready to kill because
of his frustration; now we find James at our elbow urging us to pity
Hyacinth as a passive innocent first introduced to Hoffendahl, and then
cruelly abandoned by Muniment. A Hyacinth stripped of the dignity
of his own foolish gesture of despair is embarrassingly inadequate to
the task which James assigns him in the last third of the novel. He no
longer even comes close to serving as a convincing representative of
the Jamesian value of intense consciousness. He becomes merely a
pathetically muddled young man. Schinkel, who, even though he
"lofes" Hyacinth, is placed in the novel to underline the ultimate
inhumanity of collective values, is right in spite of James when he
remarks that the revolver which Hyacinth has used "would certainly
have served much better for the Duke."

The Princess Casamassima is distinctly inferior to *The Portrait of a Lady*. Isabel's energy and self-assertiveness are real, the vital source of action in a Europe imaged in Gardencourt and Osmond's Roman villa, twin figures of lethargy, benign and sinister. Isabel wants to be free, and the force of that vague emotion is sufficient to awaken Ralph's sense of wonder and Madame Merle's rare talent for exploitation. It is also strong enough to make Isabel choose Osmond and to stir in the reader surprise and pity.

Hyacinth Robinson starts out less as the source than as the locus for action, that provided by a conflict between starkly polarized desires which are simply planted in him. At best, in Book Four, his situation is ironic and pathetic, for instead of withdrawing from the turmoil of social, political and sexual energy around him, he has pledged his life in opposition to those values of tradition and beauty which he now wants only to appreciate. He is the sensitive Jamesian observer pledged to destroy what James saw as the only objects of appreciation. His situation, dependent and passive, is intrinsically less promising than that of Isabel Archer. But when James reinforces these elements of his character in the last two books, constantly stressing the figure of Hyacinth the victim, he sacrifices whatever affective power the young man's gesture might have had. James, supposedly most free from the desire to use art for an argument, has allowed himself to be caught up in a kind of polemic: he victimizes Hyacinth in an effort to prove that the chaotic and unpredictable forces of political, social, and sexual experience inevitably trap and betray the sensitive individual. In the process of his polemic, he dissipates our interest in and sympathy for his character.

The Princess Casamassima presents us with the following paradox: on the one hand, it is a richly detailed and often plausible account of certain social forces at work in the London of the 1880's; on the other hand, the work is flawed by James's willingness to manipulate hero and milieu in an effort to prove the superior value and beauty of the sensitive, finely appreciative individual. This means preserving Hyacinth not just from the corruption, but from the passions and the risks of his society, and to the extent that James advances this Hyacinth in his argument, he loses him as a character.

4

THE SPOILS OF POYNTON

In my analysis of *The Spoils of Poynton*, I want to explore the connection between James's fascination with the aesthetic and rhetorical effects of polar design and his treatment of the moral issues raised by his heroine's story. The complex series of choices, refusals, and decisions made by Fleda Vetch is perfectly intelligible when viewed as the product of the polar conflict developed gradually throughout the novel. Fleda Vetch is the agent of this design, and her morality is equally a part of it. To put it simply, Fleda is opposed in the novel by Mrs. Gereth, a woman willing to subordinate any value to the pleasure—and for her it is intense—of having. In, and because of this opposition, Fleda is made to represent with equal intensity the value of selflessness. Thus the moral vision incorporated in the character of Fleda Vetch does not come chiefly from the author's study of the way in which manners, desires, and ethical codes are accommodated to one another in a particular society. Rather, Fleda's morality, while reasonably close to the genteel idealism theoretically approved by James's society, actually emerges from the demands of the intense conflict which James comes to think of as the essence of his story.

Our difficulty in reading the novel today is that while we are no less subject than James's contemporaries to the skill with which he evoked a response to conflict, we are more resistant to codes as rigorous as that which Fleda embodies. We particularly resist when such a code frustrates sexual satisfaction between hero and heroine after the first half of the novel has given us reasonable assurance that it is to be a comedy. The resolution of the novel has led most critics to one or the other of the following conclusions, all uncomfortable: Fleda is genuinely admirable in her idealism even though it casts Owen into a marriage which he does not want and which is sure to be bad;[1] Fleda is a mixture of strong, quite normal passion and a dangerously severe moral code, the combination making her admirable, her situation pathetic;[2] Fleda is James's portrait—whether fully intended or not we do not know—of ethical absolutism.[3]

First of all, about James's own conception of Fleda I do not think there can be any real doubt. To demonstrate the development of this conception I want to devote most of my attention to the notebook entries for the novel. They document James's search for and delighted response to the evocative design of conflict which shapes both Fleda and her morality. They are much more helpful in understanding what actually happens in the novel, and the meaning that James intends, than is the technical discussion in the Preface. James meant Fleda to appear genuinely heroic, admirable in her freedom from greed and the desire to exploit other people. He would have had little sympathy for our desire to see Fleda compromise her ideals in recognition of Owen's weakness. But this is because such a compromise would have lessened the intensity of Fleda's battle with Mrs. Gereth and what she represents. In asking James to mitigate the logic of his conclusion we ask him not just to depart from standards of his day—this he was clearly willing to do, witness *The Ambassadors;* more seriously, we ask him to qualify or simply drop the possibilities for intensity, pathos, and heroic consistency he thought inherent in his design and in the heroine he chose for it. As our analysis of the notebook entries should make clear, James would have considered the request unreasonable.

In his Preface to the novel, James spoke of Fleda Vetch as a "free spirit" in comparison with whom all the other characters in the novel appeared as fools. Fleda lacks money, family protection, and social connections. She is neither beautiful nor talented. She is, however, in James's view of her, free by virtue of her "intelligence" and her "appre-

1. Gargano, *"The Spoils,"* pp. 650-60.
2. Isle, *Experiments,* pp. 107-11.
3. Quinn, *"Morals,"* pp. 563-77.

ciation" of what goes on around her. The action of the novel is intended to isolate and dramatize the workings of Fleda's consciousness. After the fourth chapter the developments of the story are made to seem chiefly internal, the progressive movement of Fleda's judgment, loyalty, and her love for Owen Gereth. In fact, Fleda's "appreciation" of her situation, her estimate of choices available to her, and the decisions she actually makes, are all strictly dependent on the external action of the novel, chiefly on the swoops and thrusts of the embattled Mrs. Gereth. Dependent not in the obvious way—Fleda is not Mrs. Gereth's tool to be used at will—but rather by the inverse logic of James's design.

James exalts and condemns Fleda to an "appreciation" which defines itself precisely as the effort to mitigate, undo, or triumph over every act of the selfish will. She is not passive herself—nor does she lack will, as James claimed in his Preface. She fights to contain human passion, her own as well as that of others, within rational and aesthetically pleasing categories: filial love, honor, reticence, fidelity. These last are categories, ideals if we wish, and they are also Fleda's spoils, which, in the heat of the battle waged, take on a value increasingly abstracted from the human realities around her.

James wishes us to see Fleda's appreciation as splendid, and to regret that it does not prevail over the selfishness of Mona Brigstock and the weakness of Owen Gereth. But, in the process of intensifying Fleda's heroic selflessness James reifies it, leaving the reader with the uncomfortable, unintended feeling that this heroism belongs not to human beings but rather to an abstract struggle with an equally intense, equally hypothetical "selfishness." In the end, "appreciation" belongs to and depends upon this other abstraction which James makes its polar opposite, for it has outgrown the expressive capacities of a plausible character or moral scheme. The conflict in *The Spoils of Poynton*, between having and not having, reaches for an intensity which finally withers the central character.

If we carefully examine the notebook entries for *The Spoils*, and compare them with the novel itself, we can observe the way in which James's design of polar conflict first enlists our sympathy for Fleda, and then largely dissipates it by an act which is meant to be the most "sublime" expression of her appreciation and her freedom. We shall note also the difference in James's tone and preoccupations between the notebook and the Preface treatment of the novel, a difference which suggests that James's prefaces, taken by themselves, do not give us a wholly satisfactory account of his technique.

Irony is the tonal expression of James's fascination with polar conflict; paradox is the starting and ending point for all of his actions. The first notebook entry on *The Spoils of Poynton*, dated December 24, 1893, describes the donnée of his story and records a paradox different from, but related to that which James was later to discuss in his Preface. Here is the original report of the donnée from the notebook.

> Three little histories were lately mentioned to me which . . . appear worth making a note of. One of these was related to me last night at dinner at Lady Lindsay's, by Mrs. Anstruther-Thompson. It is a small and ugly matter — but there is distinctly in it, I should judge, the subject of a little tale — a little social and psychological picture.[4]

The "little history" is that of a "young laird, in Scotland," who, exercising his right under English law, has refused to allow his widowed mother to keep objects acquired by her but legally part of the son's inheritance. The mother takes all that she can carry from the ancestral home, later sends an imperious letter to the son and his new wife, demanding more.

> The son and his wife refuse, resist; the mother denounces, and (through litigation or otherwise), there is a hideous public quarrel and scandal. It has ended, my informant told me, in the mother — passionate, rebellious against her fate, resentful of the young wife and of the loss of her dignity and her home — resorting to [the] tremendous argument (though of no real *value* to her) of declaring that the young man is not the son of his putative father. (N. 137)

In the later Preface account of the donnée, what strikes James about the incident at Lady Lindsay's is the manner in which the artist must protect himself against the abundance of detail with which real life frustrates art. For his dinner companion had, it seems, tried to proceed with further details of the fight between the Scottish laird and his "passionate, rebellious" mother. Details which James, already fascinated with the incident and eager to develop a subject out of it, had to ignore. This is perhaps the most familiar account of the Jamesian donnée, and it is retold whenever critics wish to describe the discipline with which James developed his story and the rigor with which he excluded all but those elements essential to his purpose. The lesson for the Jamesian critic is that a workable subject is necessarily cut away from "clumsy life" and its distracting details.

4. *The Notebooks*, p. 136. (Since in this chapter I will make numerous references to James's notebook entries, I will use "N" with page numbers in parentheses to indicate the sources of my quotations.)

Aside from such exclusions, the original anecdote was changed, its more sensational details dropped. The Scottish laird becomes Owen Gereth. The proud and passionate woman, eventually Mrs. Gereth, fights hard but does not publicly condemn herself for adultery in order to prove her son a bastard. Fleda enters the story and James centers it in her consciousness. No Scottish lairds, violent evictions, public exposure, sexual scandal. But all of these features must have intrigued James, as well as the fact that the "sordid and ugly" little tale came to him in the flow of Lady Lindsay's dinner party. For all of these features are partially retained, James having made them less sensational, less openly violent, less shrill. James's argument for such change was that the actual eruption of violence in life, like the stream of irrelevant detail, prevents the emphasis and intensity peculiar to art.

The trick was to transmute the grand, the violent, and the scandalous into workable form. So Mrs. Gereth is not the widow of a laird, but still, through the imagery of the novel, the representative of high civilization at war with the barbarians. She identifies herself with taste and an accumulated beauty threatened by the vulgar rich with their legalistic code, the traditional weapon of the bourgeoisie and traditionally destructive of the old pieties. Lawyers and bailiffs don't enter James's version, but here again one of the chief problems posed in the donnée was that of rendering the imminence of such violence without actually letting it develop into action. James knew that the pervasive threat of violence or evil, its imaginative presence in the minds of characters trained to anticipate states of mind and passions, was more effective than the actual event. The event, however disruptive it might be, released characters and reader from anticipation into distracting reality. So in James's version the eviction doesn't actually occur, though the sense of its possibility evoked by the excited imaginations of Fleda and Mrs. Gereth allows art to do more justice to life than all the lawyers sent by the Scottish laird. Similarly, James is fascinated by, but compelled to change the detail about the mother's accusation. The charge that her son was illegitimate is hysterical and actually, as James points out, "of no real value to her." Nor is it of value to James, for it clearly expresses the release and therefore the dissipation of tension and passion.

But the notion of sex as a vehicle for the final expression of passion in a conflict between mother and son was apparently too intriguing for James to drop back into the stream of "clumsy life." Sex is a persistent theme in the novel and below the surface of events it exerts much of the pressure against which Fleda struggles. Almost from the first scene Fleda shows distaste for and bewilderment about sex, an expression of feeling which prepares her character for the final stages of the action when sex, in the hands of both Mona and Mrs. Gereth, will be made to seem the most potent weapon against the values of "appreciation" for which Fleda struggles.

What we have to recognize about James's treatment of the anecdote which provided him with his donnée for *The Spoils of Poynton* is something more than the familiar Jamesian paradox that art best renders life by rigorously stripping it of much of its detail. What is much more important in James's actual work, particularly *The Spoils of Poynton*, is the degree to which he *retained* what was bizarre, violent, and sexually sensational in the many anecdotes and subjects which he collected. Underlying Mrs. Gereth's passion is the anger of a woman, not literally an aristocrat, but an aristocrat of taste, who quite explicitly sees herself as the last real opponent of a middle-class vulgarity bent on destroying both taste and the domestic pieties. Fleda is James's extension of the original idea of embattled aristocracy: if the battle is joined over who will have the spoils, she will prove herself above having. And if sex was the last futile weapon of the woman in the anecdote, then Mrs. Gereth will urge Fleda to "let [herself] go," seduce Owen, to prevent the loss of her furniture. By refusing so stubbornly to let herself go, Fleda, in James's own mind, prevails over the final and most attractive bribe offered to this spiritual aristocrat. She maintains herself as a "free spirit." Much of what seems to be and in fact is morally inconsistent and psychologically dubious about the character of Fleda as she appears in the finished novel can be explained by gauging the residual force, for James, of that original anecdote communicated to him at Lady Lindsay's table.

The anecdote furnishes James with his chief character, the mother victimized by English law. Very soon in his thoughts about his story, he'll shift the focus and the point of view to Fleda Vetch, but it is to his first speculation about the mother that we must turn for an understanding of what he will later make of Fleda's passion. The mother's reason for desiring to keep her home and its furnishings is not simple greed or pride of ownership. The impending eviction will be made especially painful for her and interesting for James because of the keenness of her aesthetic sense. The house constitutes a symbol of a lifetime spent in devotion to art and in avid collecting. Moreover, the energy with which she resists her son is to be seen as a dramatic expression of this same aesthetic sense. Her anguish at the thought of losing her treasures generates furious energy. It makes her act. The vital principle of action in the novel is first of all a quality of mind, which is to say that James begins in *The Spoils of Poynton* with precisely the paradox which usually formed the conclusion of his novels. The truly animating forces in human experience are states of mind, qualities of consciousness rather than mundane ambition. When Fleda enters the story and becomes the most important character for James, he will begin to stress the grossly manipulative aspects of Mrs. Gereth's character, and openly acknowledge what he sometimes does not seem to recognize about the aesthetic or spiritual consciousness when it is established in the hero or heroine of his novels: that the sense of beauty or heroic idealism can exert its own coercive pressure, perhaps even more effectively than lust or greed.

Committed as he is to the infusion of states of consciousness with all the intensity of physical passion, it does not seem strange or incongruous to James that the aesthetic sense could coexist with and indeed generate a fierce combativeness: James himself, as he made his first notebook entry for *The Spoils of Poynton,* recalled the intensity with which he had recently experienced aesthetic vulgarity:

> One can imagine the rebellion, in this case (the case I should build on the above hint), of a particular sort of proud woman — a woman who had *loved* her home, her husband's home and hers (with a knowledge and adoration of artistic beauty, the tastes, the habits of a collector). There would be circumstances, details, intensifications, deepening it and darkening it all. There would be the particular type and taste of the wife the son would have chosen — a wife out of a Philistine, a tasteless, a hideous house; the kind of house the very walls and furniture of which constitute a kind of *anguish* for such a woman as I suppose the mother to be. That kind of anguish occurred to me, precisely, as a subject, during the 2 days I spent at Fox Warren (I didn't mean to write the name), a month or so ago. I thought of the strange, the terrible experience of a nature with a love and passion for beauty, united by adverse circumstances to such a family and domiciled in such a house. (N. 137)

The paradoxical fusion of the aggressive and the aesthetic is the design from which the novel begins. In the end this design will resolve itself in the disastrous fire which destroys Poynton. In the first chapter of the novel it produces comedy, the picture of Mrs. Gereth, her senses assaulted by the vulgarity of the Brigstocks' house, her nerves ragged after a night "kept awake for hours by the wallpaper in her room." Already the suspicion is beginning to dawn on her that Waterbath poses an even more serious threat than this, that the eldest of the Brigstock girls is destined to be brought home to

Poynton as her son's wife. She discovers Fleda Vetch, who is first seen as a fellow refugee in flight from vulgarity, and by the end of the chapter has been appropriated as a weapon in Mrs. Gereth's counterattack. The two women meet Owen and Mona, and on the way home Mrs. Gereth arranges for Owen to walk beside Fleda, taking charge of Mona herself.

The comedy of this first chapter is extremely engaging, James indulging himself in witty hyperbole to score off both the vulgar Brigstocks and the wounded sensibilities of Fleda and Mrs. Gereth:

> There was in [Mrs. Gereth's room] a set of comic water-colours, a family joke by a family genius, and in [Fleda's] a souvenir from some centennial or other Exhibition, that they shudderingly alluded to. The house was perversely full of souvenirs of places even more ugly than itself and of things it would have been a pious duty to forget. The worst horror was the acres of varnish, something advertised and smelly, with which everything was smeared; it was Fleda Vetch's conviction that the application of it, by their own hands and hilariously shoving each other, was the amusement of the Brigstocks on rainy days.[5]

However brilliant this first chapter may be, it is, in the context of the whole novel, rather misleading. The fact is that we are not intended to follow the lead of James's tone here and regard vulgarity and exquisite taste as about equally amusing. Nor should we consider Mrs. Gereth's intervention at the end of the chapter to pair off Fleda and Owen as simply an interested mother's contrivance of what should come about anyway between the hero and the heroine of a novel. If Mrs. Gereth's aestheticism is seen as wholly absurd, then we have difficulty explaining Fleda's initial reaction to Poynton and her subsequent allegiance to Mrs. Gereth in defense of her possessions. Mrs. Gereth's aestheticism is later made to seem inferior in value to Fleda's heroic idealism, but never so ridiculous as the tone of this first chapter makes it seem.

> Their drawing room, Mrs. Gereth lowered her voice to mention, caused her face to burn, and each of the new friends confided to the other that in her own apartment she had given way to tears. (7)

And, as we shall learn from both the notebook entries and the finished version of the novel, the chief reason why, in James's mind, the satisfactory resolution of Fleda's love for Owen is impossible was that this love was promoted—as its initial stages were promoted—by Mrs. Gereth. It is of the essence of Fleda's character that she serves higher gods than those of Mrs. Gereth. Owen is Mrs. Gereth's possession, her

5. James, *The Spoils*, p. 7.

bribe to Fleda, the human surrogate of the spoils themselves. What seems in the last scene of Chapter One to be a pleasant if bluntly engineered beginning of the love relationship contains the seed of Fleda's "heroic" renunciation of that relationship on any except her own impossibly high terms.

In the second notebook entry, dated May 13, 1895, James still hopes to condense his treatment of the subject into a play and has projected three "acts." The marriage between the son, at this point called Albert, and the vulgar Brigstock, is to take place in Act I. In Act II, the mother effects what James called the "despoiling" of her home, seizing the goods and retreating to the small cottage to be called Ricks in the finished version. In Act III, the sensitive girl, here "Muriel," takes the field in an attempt to get the mother to make restitution. She does this, notes James, because she "secretly loves the young man." She will succeed, James says, but the fire at the dénouement of this act destroys the house and all Mrs. Gereth's possessions.

At this point in James's plans, Fleda, originally introduced as a counterbalance to the son's wife, is becoming more important as an agent. There is no question, however, of her love for Owen Gereth succeeding. Its very existence seems clearly designed to make more affecting, more distinguished, her efforts in support of Owen's cause, now of course equally the cause of his wife. The love between hero and heroine is thus from the very first relegated to the sphere of sacrifice, tribute to a lover safely beyond attainment. Act III, in this version, is clearly a thematic counterpoise to Act II, the ethic of heroic self-sacrifice figuring for James as sufficiently contrary to Mrs. Gereth's seizure of Act II. The hopeless little passion, easily convertible *in James's mind* to reunuciation of *possible* marriage, transcends Mrs. Gereth's passionate, selfish will.

In the novel Fleda prefers to risk losing Owen rather than take him before he has been explicitly released by Mona. We are allowed to presume that without such a release there can be no marriage. Most modern critics of the novel, whatever their ultimate judgment of it may be, take this stand of Fleda's as crucial to the moral vision of the book. It is crucial, I think, but for two other reasons: it is the most dramatic expression of the lengths to which the design of the novel drives its heroine in her opposition to Mrs. Gereth; it is the point of maximum strain upon the reader's belief and sympathy. Fleda, who enters the novel as a check against uncompromising greed, here takes a stand opposed to Mrs. Gereth's in every way, except in its refusal to make a concession to Owen's weakness. But the key point to note is that James never even considered marriage between Fleda and Owen as a real possibility. Their love was from its beginning in James's mind a difficulty to be overcome by Fleda in her progress toward heroism.

The evidence of both the notebook entries and the finished novel clearly indicates that James had no thought of submitting Fleda Vetch to something so ordinary as conflict with another woman over a man. In the early stages of James's planning, Owen has already been taken. In the finished version we are made to believe that Fleda could easily take him away from Mona if she chose. In the entry of August 11, 1895, James seems eager to prevent Fleda from falling into banal competition with Mona. Here he considers the scene in which Owen proudly brings Mona to Poynton. Fleda, whom James never allows a straightforward understanding of Mona's sexual attraction, is puzzled over the young man's obvious devotion to Mona. But "it is only *for* Mrs. Gereth that Fleda is, as it were, jealous; she says, in the face of Mona: 'Good heavens, if she were *my* mother, how common and stupid she would make, in comparison and contrast, such a girl as that, appear!' " (N. 207)

The most important advance in this entry is James's decision to make Mrs. Gereth actively thrust forth Fleda Vetch as her personal candidate for Owen's hand and her possessions.

> Owen shows himself to his mother *and* Fleda in the morning; and Fleda, after a vision of what is going on between them, goes out, leaves them together. She goes out into the grounds and finds Mona there; ten words about what passes between the 2 women. They come in again, and then it is that Fleda has the sense of what Mrs. G. has said to Owen — has probably, dreadfully said — about her. . . .
> It is then — after [Owen and the Brigstocks] are gone — that Mrs. Gereth lets [Fleda] know or suspect, to her horror, what she has already seemed to divine, to apprehend — that she *did* speak (while F. was in the garden with M.) about her, F., being *her* ideal for a daughter-in-law. (N. 208-09)

In the novel James doubly emphasizes the importance of this development by rendering Mrs. Gereth's announcement in a dramatic scene, in the midst of which Fleda runs away in shame, but only to imagine, with the reader, that Mrs. Gereth is making even more emphatic her offer to Owen inside the house. Mrs. Gereth, in the dramatized portion of the scene, is splendidly histrionic. She speaks of what her possessions have meant to her and her husband:

> "They were our religion, they were our life, they were *us!* And now they're only *me* — except that they're also *you,* thank God, a little, you dear!" she continued, suddenly inflicting on Fleda a kiss intended by every sign to knock her into position. . . .

"They're living things to me; they know me, they return the touch of my hand. But I could let them all go, since I have to so strangely, to another affection, another conscience. . . . Rather than make them over to a woman ignorant and vulgar I think I'd deface them with my own hands." (30-31)

Shortly after this scene Fleda herself confronts Mrs. Gereth and notifies her of "her instant departure: she couldn't possibly remain after being offered to Owen so distinctly, before her very face, as his mother's candidate for the honour of his hand." (33) But stay she does,

> taking refuge in the thin comfort of the truth at least brought home to her. The truth was simply that all Mrs. Gereth's scruples were on one side and that her ruling passion had in a manner despoiled her of her humanity. On the second day, when the tide of emotion had somewhat ebbed, she said soothingly to her companion: "But you *would,* after all, marry him, you know, darling, wouldn't you, if that girl were not there? I mean of course if he were to ask you," Mrs. Gereth had thoughtfully added. . . .
>
> "Marry him if he were to ask me? Most distinctly not!" (37-38)

This is the second scene dominated by Mrs. Gereth's desire to pair her son with a woman who would make a good custodian for Poynton. Whereas Fleda was merely amused at Mrs. Gereth's contrivance in Chapter One, she is here very ashamed. Nothing in the text or in any of James's commentaries on his story indicates that the author thinks this reaction strange or overly delicate. On the contrary, James thinks it quite reasonable that Fleda should resist Mrs. Gereth's interference so vehemently, and he subsequently regards this very resistance as perfectly legitimate motivation for Fleda's very intricate efforts to prevent Mrs. Gereth from learning of first her love and then Owen's. There is no evidence within the novel to indicate that James judged Fleda's delicacy excessive. It accompanies her sensitive moral intuition, and like the latter is for James an inextricable part of her fine appreciation of what is taking place around her. The scene I have just quoted from foreshadows and serves the same rhetorical function as the later scene in which Mrs. Gereth sees Fleda off for London with the advice that she seek out Owen and "let [herself] go." However much pleasure we may take from the rhetoric of Mrs. Gereth's speech, we are intended to see it as a serious encroachment upon Fleda's rights as a person, a disdain for the delicacy of her feelings, and, in a very muted but still perceptible way, Mrs. Gereth's offer of sexual rights to Fleda in return for the mother's continued possession of her objects. That Fleda herself is portrayed in the novel as being in love with Owen makes little difference to James after this. For Fleda is conceived of as the opposite, ultimately the negation of Mrs. Gereth's selfish will, and consequently she must be prepared to take Owen on none other but her own terms. That those terms prove too high shows only that Fleda's "appreciation" is pathetically, even tragically for James, isolated in her milieu.

We have observed a pattern emerging as James plans his heroine's relations with Owen Gereth, and that pattern is faithfully reproduced in the finished novel. The relationship is to be complicated from beginning to end by the uses which Mrs. Gereth is prepared to make of it, and by the answering strategy by which Fleda attempts to hide the truth about her feelings and thus protect herself. As we shall discover, Fleda is never allowed by James to deal with Owen apart from the use his mother makes of him in her attempt to secure the spoils. As a matter of fact, he is invested by both women with an emblematic significance. He comes to stand for the spoils, an inducement to Fleda to give in to the older woman. And despite the extended *scène de passion* which James finally gives us toward the end of the novel, the design of the novel requires that Fleda *act* toward Owen as a surrogate for the spoils, rather than simply as her lover. She poses a condition for accepting him which is so unlikely to be satisfied as to prove that she, Fleda, can be as intense in her sacrifice as Mrs. Gereth is in her greed. On the other hand, if we judge Fleda's act from a moral standpoint we are surely bound to note she fails utterly to make the simple distinction between an act that may be good in itself and the selfish motives of someone else who recommends it.

The problem for the reader is that he is not quite so willing as the two women to regard Owen as emblem for the spoils in the novel's polar design. For by making Owen substantial enough that sacrificing him reflects credit on Fleda, James makes him solid enough for the reader to wish that he be taken or rejected on his own realistic merits.

By the time James made his third notebook entry (October 15, 1895), Fleda's consciousness had been established as the center of the story. Here, he sketches out the scene in which Fleda comes from London to Ricks to discover that Mrs. Gereth has transported all of her possessions from Poynton. Since Fleda now figures much more importantly in the story than Mrs. Gereth, it is necessary for James to find a complication, a situation that will be for her "sufficiently intense and sufficiently determining." He finds it in the idea that Owen will reciprocate Fleda's love.

I had intended to make Fleda 'fall in love' with Owen, or, to express it *moins banalement,* to represent her as loving him. But I had not intended to represent a feeling of this kind on Owen's part. Now, however, I have done so; in my last little go at the thing (which I have been able to do only so interruptedly), it inevitably took that turn and I must accept the idea and work it out. What I felt to be necessary, as the turn in question came, was that what should happen between Fleda and Owen Gereth should be something of a certain intensity. (N. 214)

The new intensity results first of all not in any thought of eventual marriage, that being sufficiently ruled out by Mrs. Gereth's desire for it, but rather in Fleda's suffering for the wrong that is being done Owen, and her renewed desire to get his property back for him.

What has happened makes her think only of Owen. His marriage hasn't as yet taken place, but it's near at hand — it's there. She expects nothing more from him — has a dread of its happening. She wants only, as she believes, or tries to believe, never to see him again. She surrenders him to Mona. She has a dread of his not doing his duty — backing out in any way. That would fill her with horror and dismay. (N. 215)

With this dread of Owen's doing anything but his duty and marrying Mona, Fleda, in James's projection of his action, goes down to Ricks where she discovers that Mrs. Gereth has ransacked Poynton.

The light on Mrs. Gereth's action, however, that she encounters at Ricks, changes the whole situation; causes her to hold her breath — making her not know exactly WHAT may happen. Now, *voyons un peu, mon bon:* the whole idea of my thing is that Fleda becomes rather fine, DOES something, distinguishes herself (to the reader), and that this is really almost all that has made the little anecdote worth telling at all. . . . What I have seen Fleda do is operate successfully (to state it as broadly as possible), to the end that the things be mainly sent back to Poynton. (N. 215)

Facing the problem of how Fleda is to manage this, James remarks that whereas he had before intended to have the young girl persuade Mrs. Gereth to make restitution, "now that the emotion [Fleda's love] is developed more and Owen himself is made, as it were, active, I feel as if I wanted something more—I don't know what to call it except *dramatic.*" (N. 215)

Fleda will act; her resolution of the conflict will be both heroic and dramatic. With the knowledge that she has only to do nothing to secure for herself Poynton and Owen Gereth, Fleda will act to ensure that she obtains neither. For Owen is now, in James's mind, identified with the spoils by virtue of the fact that both are manipulated by Mrs. Gereth and both function dramatically as temptations to Fleda.

[Owen] is thrust by his mother into danger again. Mrs. Gereth is operating with so much more inflammable material than she knows. . . . If I want *beauty* for [Fleda] — beauty of action and poetry of effect, I can only, I think, find it just there; find it in making her heroic. To *be* heroic, to achieve beauty and poetry, she must conceal from [Owen] what she feels. . . . What does she do then? — how does she work, how does she achieve her heroism? She does it in the first and highest way by urging him on to his marriage — putting it before him that it must take place without a week's more delay. (N. 216-17)

James is now in full possession of his subject, his dramatic design. And Fleda, in James's projection of his story, has been transformed from a plausible character, autonomous and well developed enough to bear analysis of her motives, into an agent of James's design. She entered James's conception of the story as a counterpoise to the vulgar fiancée of the son. She grew into a weapon, soon the chief weapon in Mrs. Gereth's strategy. James, initially attracted by the paradoxical fusion of the aesthetic and the violent in Mrs. Gereth's character, moved to the conception of Fleda's consciousness as the radical opposite of the older woman's fierce possessiveness. Fleda will distinguish herself by a selflessness which, if it is not so fierce as Mrs. Gereth's quality, is more ingenious and more obdurate. Fleda will *act* not to have, and in order that this action might display beauty and intensity, she will be depicted as deeply desiring that which it is her role as agent in the action to renounce. Her love for Owen Gereth is, for James, from the very first of his speculation about his subject, a measure of the temptation to be overcome in her assertion of an ideal opposite to that which drives Mrs. Gereth. From this point on, every action of Fleda's which might at first seem inexplicable, or the product of a perverse desire to frustrate her own happiness and Owen's, should instead be seen by the reader as an expression of Fleda's heroism, her attainment, through James's design, of the status of "free spirit." For example, in this same entry of October 15, James notes that in entering into a bargain with Owen by which she agrees to regain the spoils and he agrees to go through with his marriage, Fleda knows that Owen no longer even likes Mona.

(Fleda, by the way, has coerced Owen into this agreement, or transaction, as I call it, by being in possession — entering into possession — of his secret, as it were, without having surrendered to him her own. This secret of his change about Mona is *used* by her in her 'heroism.') (N. 218)

James seems clearly to have been very far removed from the thought that Owen Gereth's interests might not be best served by heroism of this kind. Fleda is equally free of such doubt.

James's notebook entry dated February 13, 1896, furthers his conception of Fleda's heroism, indicates something of the rhetorical effect he intends to gain from the love between Owen and Fleda, and answers several questions about the novel which have troubled critics. Even at this late point when the character of Owen has taken over from the spoils much of their aura of a glittering bribe, James does not want to forsake the things themselves as an element in Fleda's temptation. Nor, of course, does he wish to ignore Mrs. Gereth's role as Fleda's personal and ethical antagonist. His comments in the entry make this clear and also give us an answer to a perplexing question about Mrs. Gereth's motivation: why does so shrewd a tactician send back her possessions on what seems to be, after all, such flimsy evidence of Fleda's eventual success?

> Mrs. Gereth surrenders the things partly because she believes — has reason to — that Fleda will eventually come into them. But that calculation won't — doesn't — appear a sufficient motive: she must have another to strengthen it. She surrenders them therefore, furthermore, because she appears to see that the knowledge of their being back again at Poynton, as an incentive, a heritage, a reward, a future (settled there again immutably, this time), will operate to make Fleda do what she has so passionately appealed to her to do — get Mona away from Owen. (N. 248)

It is also in this entry and the following one, dated February 19, that James sketches in the *scène de passion* which will eventually take place in Chapter Nineteen of the novel. Here Fleda finally "breaks down," lets fall her pretence of mere friendship for Owen, and openly declares her love. Since the scene is the most explicit rendering of romantic passion to be found in James, it is easy to misread. The wrong way to view the scene is to suppose that here at last the emotions of a young woman overwhelm an impossibly rigorous, if abstractly admirable, moral code; that here at last what is distinctly human and free about Fleda Vetch is allowed to fight through the surface laid down by her conscience and her delicacy. James sees the scene in quite a different manner, a fact which three details from his notebooks make perfectly clear.

First of all, although Fleda does break down at this point, James sees this as a flaw in her heroism rather than as the emergence of feelings stronger than ideals. Fleda will slip once again before the end of the novel, when she sends a telegram to Owen asking him to come to her although Fleda knows he is at Waterbath at her command. Secondly, even though James here allows his heroine to reveal the secret she has so passionately guarded, he does not allow either her

or Owen to take the responsibility for breaking an engagement which
is now a mockery. Mona must break, and since Mona, like Mrs.
Gereth, is identified as implacable will, Fleda is in no real danger of
relinquishing her heroism merely for the sake of, at last, taking Owen.

> Fleda breaks down — lets Owen see she loves him. It is all *covert* —
> and delicate and exquisite: she adjures him to do his literal duty to
> Mona. They arrive at some definite and sincere agreement about this.
> That is the ground, the *fond,* the deep ground TONE of their scene. It
> must be for MONA to break — only for Mona. (N. 249)

> Fleda's *aveux* are all qualified — saddened and refined, and made *beau-
> tiful,* by the sense of the IMPOSSIBLE — the sense of the infinite
> improbability of Mona's not really hanging on — and by the perfectly
> firm and definite ground she takes on the absolute demand of Owen's
> honour that he shall go on with Mona if she DOESN'T break. (N. 254)

. The scene is beautifully typical of James's intention in this novel
and in much of his work. Outwardly it is perfectly familiar to novel-
readers of the period, for which reason James first thinks of it by its
generic name, "the *scène de passion.*" "Yes," says James, "I must give
my readers that." The scene, exploiting the customary reactions of
readers, allows us to look forward to a resolution of the novel which, if
not perfectly satisfactory, would at least satisfy the emotions which
both characters express in the scene. But James wishes us, in the
process of granting the genuineness of this type of passion, to recognize that its satisfaction would render impossible a higher beauty and
a greater intensity. That intensity results from Fleda's utter fidelity to
the ethic of selflessness. The *scène de passion* is intended to be less a
demonstration of Fleda's capacity for human love than a sign of her
ability to achieve something which James regarded as more distinguished. The scene functions rhetorically not to awaken in the
reader an expectation of an eventual compromise between Fleda's
principles and her love, but rather to certify those principles by making us feel how much Fleda must forgo in order to abide by them.
James's action has made of her a free spirit; it frees her to triumph
over desire as thoroughly and as intensely as the fire consumes the
spoils at the end of the novel.

I have tried to demonstrate in my analysis of *The Spoils of
Poynton,* the manner in which James used the relationship between
Fleda and Owen Gereth to subserve the strict demands of the novel's
design. The relationship itself, as we have seen from the Notebook
entries, originated in James's desire to intensify Fleda's situation and
her struggle by providing her with the opportunity of giving up not

only the spoils, but Owen, their human representative. This development of Owen as a surrogate for the things strikes James as an extremely effective strategy for ensuring that Fleda will appear pathetic and heroic to the reader, as extraordinary in her willingness to forgo as Mrs. Gereth is in her desire to take. For James, then, Fleda's reaction to Owen is only the most dramatic and evocative expression of her selflessness, a quality which, following the logic of his design, James has made as extreme as Mrs. Gereth's greed.

But for the reader, the character of Owen has acquired something more than an emblematic identity. For all his faults, he strikes us as too solid and substantial a character to be so totally absorbed into the schematic, fierce, but oddly abstract conflict between the two women. To be sure, Owen is clumsy, indecisive, a hopeless mixture of good impulses and muddled thought. His relationship with Fleda is hectic and disjointed and, were it to evolve into marriage, would clearly offer little of the rigorous consistency of which Fleda, acting by herself, is capable. But the relationship, with all its tendency toward comic confusion, insinuates into the novel a degree of warmth and energy which, behind James's back, wars against the inflexible logic by which the author intends to work out Fleda's story.

In the end, the reader resists James's efforts to dispose of Owen and resolve the sexual theme of the novel as mere ingredients in his drama of conflict between extremes of greed and selflessness. Here James's pursuit of his design has forced his heroine to attack, or if we prefer, to rise above one of the principal sources of her credibility and of the reader's sympathy for her. The result in the reader is doubt, resistance to claims made by the author for his heroine's "sublimity."

In considering the relation between the Jamesian design and the author's status as pyschologist, social critic, and moralist, we have had numerous occasions to consider his treatment of sexuality. In *The Portrait of a Lady, The Princess Casamassima,* and *The Spoils of Poynton* we have noted the use made of this theme to support and intensify the drama of polar conflict. We ought now to look at a novel in which the theme is centrally focused by James's design: *The Awkward Age.*

5

THE AWKWARD AGE

In an essay on the work of Gabriele D'Annunzio, James criticized the novelist for his inadequate representation of sexual passion.

That sexual passion . . . insists on remaining for him *only* the act of a moment, beginning and ending in itself and disowning any representative character. From the moment it depends on itself alone for its beauty it endangers extremely its distinction, so precarious at the best. For what it represents, precisely, is it poetically interesting; it finds its extension and consummation only in the rest of life. Shut out from the rest of life . . . it has no more dignity than . . . the boots and shoes . . . in the corridors of promiscuous hotels. . . . What the participants do with their agitation, in short, or even what it does with them, *that* is the stuff of poetry. . . .[1]

To understand James's own treatment in *The Awkward Age* of the "poetically interesting" passion, we need to recall what the characters in novels already discussed have done with their agitation, and what it has done with them. Isabel resists the sexuality of Caspar Goodwood, refusing the escape it offers from the somber consistency of return to Osmond. Sexuality, in James's eyes, threatens what his

1. James, *Selected Literary Criticism*, p. 295.

87

heroine has achieved. As for Hyacinth Robinson, his disillusionment and betrayal are effected in great part by the random sexuality of the Princess Casamassima. The jealousy he experiences as he stands with the hapless Prince and watches her and Paul Muniment enter a house together is akin to that of a child denied the maternal love and protection he wants. Fleda Vetch encounters in Mona Brigstock, but cannot comprehend, a blunt physical force which finally knocks Owen into place. James remarks that Mona is all will, and her sexuality is merely the physical extension of that will. On the other hand, Fleda's own passionate declaration of love and desire for Owen comes only after she and her creator have made the satisfaction of this desire impossible. Her sexuality is intended to enhance the victory she achieves over it, to evoke pathos for the loss of that which James carefully keeps beneath her reach, and to beguile the reader. But most of all, as in the case of Isabel Archer, James's treatment of sexual passion is intended to certify the value of an alternative, a richer experience.

It is fair to say, then, that while James depended in his novels upon moral conventions erected by society on the base of sexuality, he nevertheless regarded the satisfaction of sexual desire as at least a hindrance to the attainment of an experience that would be intense, tragic, or transformative. James's fiercely cherished belief in a radical spiritual individualism, his celebration of the isolated, intense consciousness, finds expression in his plots in a persistent attack on the social and literary ideal of union, the most obvious form of which was marriage and sexuality. In this respect he played an intricate double game as an artist. He contrived on the one hand to arouse our sympathy for his heroes and heroines who either fail to achieve union or are tortured by it. But at the same time, he fosters in us the conviction that union, if ever fully and satisfactorily achieved, would inevitably lessen the brilliance of his character's experience. Marriage in general, and not just the one entered into by Verena Tarrant, was most apt to be "far from brilliant," and James wished to depict the brilliant. Of his major works of fiction only in *The Golden Bowl* is the effect of brilliance made to arise out of the fact of marriage; even here the marriage, reconstructed from the fragments of adultery, is singularly the creation of the heroine, Maggie Verver. Her husband figures as the most important piece, but a piece nonetheless, of this creation.

A number of critics, among whom the most helpful are Leon Edel and S. Gorley Putt, have commented on James's reluctance to see marriage and sexuality as equal to his own or his heroes' desire for experience.[2] But the point may be pursued a bit further. If the attainment of the most intense and therefore valuable states of consciousness is not served, is indeed threatened by marriage and the sexual relation, we might ask how far we are justified in assuming that James's English novels of the nineties are primarily dramatic critiques of a society's failure to establish or adhere to conventions which facilitate such union. Specifically, we ought to reexamine our habit of regarding these works as ironic portraits of the excesses and abuses of late Victorian society. It seems to me a good deal more just, given James's suspicion of marriage and sex, which pervades the work of over fifty years, to suppose that James found in the nineties in the upper middle-class phenomenon of adultery what he had before found in the figure of the fortune hunter lying in wait for the American heiress: a convenient means for articulating his sense of the hazards posed by marriage or indeed any form of sexual passion.

The opposition between sex and consciousness is a constant in James's work. It is yet another manifestation of that design of polarity which we have discovered at the heart of James's conception of Isabel Archer, Hyacinth Robinson and Fleda Vetch, and in the action with which James both reveals and develops these characters. We are surely meant to feel sympathy for a character like Maisie Farange as she attempts to defend herself in the midst of the most flagrant sexual irresponsibility in the adults who gather around her. That is, James is perfectly willing to exploit our feeling that a society so lacking in self-restraint must be corrupt. But, if we content ourselves with the belief that the focus of the novel is the tension between a child's innocence and a society's corruption, we sacrifice much of this extraordinary achievement, and all of what is most characteristically Jamesian about it. The novel is in fact based upon the radical opposition between consciousness, dramatically heightened by being treated at its emergent stages, and sexual passion. The basic technique which governs this conflict and our response to it is the simple reversal of the values and emotional qualities which the middle-class reader can be expected to associate with the experiences of knowledge and passion. Maisie learns to distinguish between power and beauty—the novel is about the process by which she comes to know—and to this experience of learning James imparts all of the excitement, passion, and what I can only call intense self-realization, that the post-romantic bourgeois associates with sexual passion. On the other hand, the affairs of the adults in the novel are, through James's management of his action and scenes,

2. Edel, *Conquest of London*, pp. 350-59, 407-17. Putt, *Henry James*, pp. 265-307.

made comic in their pretensions to passion by their very rigid regularity, their abstract and abstracting precision. Their adulteries resemble the perfectly lucid stages of a trivial and familiar argument. The audacity and the passion belong to Maisie and James. The adults get in and out of bed to a pedantic rhythm made even more ridiculous by their little cries of pleasure. If it is true that her real and foster parents compromise the child, then it is even truer to the novel's basic intent to say that Maisie's "little passion" more deeply compromises the sexuality which the adults in the novel are so mockingly made to represent.

The Awkward Age is another novel which we have often misread by attending too closely to what we take to be social satire and thus failing to grasp the use to which James has put the theme of sexuality in his design of polar conflict. The corruption of the times is not so much James's subject as it is the pretext for, and the instrument of an opposition between two forms of sexuality to which his imagination returned over and over again throughout his career, but particularly during the nineties. The essential conflict in the novel is between Mrs. Brookenham and her daughter Nanda. The conflict enables James to give his most thorough and neatly balanced treatment to his concept of sex as, on the one hand, the source of pragmatically effective energy and action and as, on the other hand, vulnerability, exposure.

This last idea finds expression in Nanda Brookenham as well as in Maisie, to some extent in Fleda Vetch, in the pupil in the story of that name, and in many other of James's characters of the period. The singular appeal of the concept of sex as exposure lies somewhat deeper than our immediate moral response: that the innocent and the helpless ought to be protected from the powerful and irresponsible. Forced by James's technique into prolonged speculation about exactly what Maisie knows, how much Nanda has been tainted, what Miles and his sister have been told by Peter Quint, the reader may grope toward the safety of complete sympathy for the exposed innocent, and equally emphatic disdain for the aggressive adult. Such a reaction is safe for the reader since it relieves our tendency, subtly encouraged by such prolonged and intense speculation over the possibility of corruption, to desire that corruption, if only to ease the strain. To the extent that we harbor a wish that the prolonged tension of exposure may be resolved, even by what the novel forces us to call the corruption of the innocent, to that extent do we accord these heroines, Nanda, Maisie, and the rest, our slightly guilty and therefore fervent sympathy and approval. The strategy at work at the root of James's studies of innocence threatened by prolonged exposure to sex is a much more subtle but not essentially dissimilar method from that used by Richardson. We are teased into fascinated interest and when we find ourselves desiring that which is so ominously and persistently possible, we then recoil into the safety of moral judgments about corrupt societies. These judgments may be true to the work, but they do not adequately describe it.

It seems clear to me that the idea of sexual exposure exerted some such effect on James, and he in turn contrives to produce the effect in the reader. And nowhere does this effect succeed so well as in *The Awkward Age,* James's study of the conflict between a sexually mature, flamboyantly exposed mother, and her threatened, sadly knowledgeable, but still virginal daughter. The aggressive force which derives from sexuality is not here diffused throughout a number of adults, as in *What Maisie Knew.* Nor is the innocent accorded some desire or capacity to act for herself in opposition to and outside the play of sexual forces around her, as in the case of Isabel Archer or Milly Theale. Aggressor and innocent are made to confront one another directly. The characters are about equally matched so far as the evocative power they embody is concerned. In them James deals most directly with "sexual passion" that "finds its extension and consummation . . . in the rest of life."

The main lines of the story in *The Awkward Age* are clear enough, although the antecedent action and the motives of the principals are in some ways obscure. Mr. Longdon, a comfortably wealthy gentleman from the country, arrives in London to make the acquaintance of Mrs. Fernanda Brookenham, whose mother Mr. Longdon had loved as a youth. He finds Mrs. Brookenham the chief luminary of a small but at least verbally brilliant social circle, an attractive and clever woman with the power to command the extravagant allegiance of the members of her group. Two of her most devoted subjects are Vanderbank and Mr. Mitchett (Mitchy), desirable ornaments for her drawing room not only for their wit but for their eligibility. Mitchy is exceedingly ugly, good-natured, rich beyond a mother's dream. Vanderbank is genteelly poor, but possessed of a charm which the other members of the circle call "the sacred terror," a powerful attractive force the exact nature of which eludes the reader.

Mr. Longdon enters this circle in time to observe Mrs. Brook as she attempts to meet a formidable social challenge. Her daughter Nanda has reached the age at which unmarried girls are customarily "brought downstairs" into the society which is expected to launch them, with as little awkwardness and as much speed as possible, into marriage. Mrs. Brook's problem is twofold: Nanda's charms, although quite real, do not include either beauty or wealth, London's accredited currency, and so it seems likely that Nanda's stay in her mother's drawing room will be embarrassingly prolonged. But this means that Mrs. Brook's circle must be deprived of certain conversational staples, considered unsuitable for a girl. Mrs. Brook must somehow manage to exhibit and thereby marry her daughter and at the same time preserve freedom of conversation in her drawing room. Her plan, it develops, is to dispatch Nanda into the arms of Mitchy's fortune, but in this she is thwarted by her cousin, the Duchess, whose daughter Aggie has apparently not been exposed to adult society, and by Nanda herself. Nanda persuades Mitchy to marry Aggie. (Walter Isle, in his discussion of *The Awkward Age,* remarks that the names of the characters, "if repeated often enough, begin to sound pretty silly."[3] This may, as Isle suggests, "reflect James's attitude toward the society," but also the pointedly childish nicknames assigned to the characters reinforce the reader's sense that one of James's most persistent interests in sex was its effect upon children and adolescents.)

Mr. Longdon, infatuated with Nanda—or at least that part of her that evokes memories of the once beloved Lady Julia—and appalled by Mrs. Brook, throws his fortune into the game by offering Vanderbank money if he will marry Nanda. Van is the girl's choice also, but he, for reasons that have perplexed almost every critic of the novel, refuses to act. Mrs. Brook, correctly assuming that Mr. Longdon will go to any lengths to remove Nanda from what he regards as the contaminating presence of her group, effects this solution with a vivid demonstration of just how bad her influence is. Nanda, after one last fruitless attempt to stir Vanderbank to action, retires to the uncomplicated countryside, to the haven of Mr. Longdon's estate and the security of his protection. We are not precisely sure at the end of the novel whether she is to be his ward or his wife, but at any rate she has passed through her mother's drawing room.

In the Preface to *The Awkward Age,* James divides his attention between the social origins and implications of his subject and the structural techniques by which it was implemented. First, he surveys the manner in which various nations deal with the problems posed by the emergence of the young girl into society. The French simply closet the *jeune fille* until marriage dispels the need for ignorance and she

3. Isle. *Experiments,* pp. 169-70.

may take her place in a drawing room whose conversation knows no limits beyond the wit of its patrons. The Americans defer absolutely to the innocence of the maiden and strive to incorporate it into the national character. The English, it seemed to James, had no system at all, but the happy facility for confounding inconsistency with compromise. The young girl is to be launched, her innocence is to be scrupulously preserved, and at the same time there is to be no abatement of "good talk." James remarks how the muddle works to his advantage, for it offers him as a subject "the failure of successful arrangement" and "the fruits of compromise." The rhythm of a social ideal is upset by the insistent claims of the special case.

> The Awkward Age is precisely a study of one of these curtailed or extended periods of tension and apprehension, an account of the manner in which the resented interference with ancient liberties came to be in a particular instance dealt with.[4]

In the second half of the Preface, James discusses the structure of the novel, the manner in which he has surrounded his subject with a series of " 'social occasion[s]' in the history and intercourse of the characters concerned."[5]

> The beauty of the conception was in this approximation of the respective divisions of my form to the successive Acts of a Play. . . .[6]

He prides himself on having achieved a perfectly scenic presentation, never being forced to narrate directly what is going on in the minds of his characters or outside the place in which his scenes are rendered.

> To make the presented occasion tell all its story itself, remain shut up in its own presence and yet on that patch of staked-out ground become thoroughly interesting and remain thoroughly clear, is a process not remarkable, no doubt, so long as a very light weight is laid on it, but difficult enough to challenge and inspire great adroitness so soon as the elements to be dealt with begin at all to 'size up.'[7]

James's own emphasis in the Preface to The Awkward Age offers the critic the greatest possible justification for a study of the social themes of the novel and of its technique. On the other hand, the Preface appears to offer little encouragement to a study which locates conflict beneath the level of social intercourse, in the polarity exhibited by antagonistic forms of sexuality. To show that the latter approach is not so fanciful as it might seem from a study of James's Preface, I

4. Art of the Novel, p. 103.
5. Ibid., p. 110.
6. Ibid.
7. Ibid., p. 111.

want once again to contrast his notebook entry with the author's commentary in his Preface. There is only one entry for the novel listed in the collection edited by Matthiessen, and it is comparatively short. The date under which it appears is March 4, 1895.

> The idea of the little London girl who grows up to 'sit with' the free-talking modern young mother—reaches 17, 18, etc.—comes out—and, not marrying, has to 'be there'—and, though the conversation is supposed to be expurgated for her, inevitably hears, overhears, guesses, follows, takes in, becomes acquainted with, horrors. A real little subject in this, I think—a real little situation for a short tale—if circumstance and setting is really given it. A young man who likes her—wants to take her out of it—feeling how she's exposed, etc. Attitude of the mother, the father, etc. The young man hesitates, because he thinks she already knows too much; but all the while he hesitates she knows, she learns, more and more. He finds out sómehow how much she *does* know, and terrified at it, drops her: all her ignorance, to his sense, is gone. His attitude to her mother—whom he has liked, visited, talked freely with, taken pleasure in. But when it comes to taking *her* daughter—! She has appealed to him to do it—begged him to take her away. 'Oh, if some one would only marry her. I know—I have a bad conscience about her.' She may be an ugly one—who has also a passion for the world—for life—likes to be there—to hear, to know. There may be the contrasted clever, *avisée* foreign or foreignized friend or sister, who has married her daughter, very virtuously and very badly, unhappily, just to get her out of the atmosphere of her own talk and entourage—and takes *my* little lady to task for her inferior system and inferior virtue. Something in this really, I think—especially if one makes it take in something of the question of the non-marrying of girls, the desperation of mothers, the whole alteration of manners—in the sense of the *osé*—and tone, while our theory of the participation, the *presence* of the young, remains unaffected by it. Then the type of the little girl who is conscious and aware. 'I am modern—I'm supposed to know—I'm not a *jeune fille*,' etc.[8]

What appears first to have attracted James's interest was the idea of the young girl "in the midst of horrors." Though the horrors were to be muted by their context, a London drawing room, the shock of the girl's exposure was to be intensified by her acute awareness of her surroundings. She "hears, overhears, guesses, follows, takes in, becomes acquainted with." Already James seems pointed toward the paradox with which he heightened the story of Maisie's exposure: the very element of corruption, the horrors which threaten the young girl, serve as a stimulus not to an awakening sexuality but rather to a curiously abstract passion for awareness, a consciousness of one's surroundings so acute as to partially redeem the sordidness on which it

8. *The Notebooks,* p. 192.

feeds. Sex is to be, even at this stage of his donnée, the unexplored territory through which the mind of the innocent picks its way toward a richer passion. Sex for the child and adolescent heroines of this period bears a considerable resemblance to the "Europe" of Isabel Archer, Strether, and Milly Theale.

James's innocent established among "horrors" evokes the idea of a young man suitably qualified to rescue her. James checks this idea, however, with a plan to make Vanderbank at first disposed to save the girl from corruption, and then disposed to reject her for the taint which she has presumably acquired. I think it virtually certain that James thought of this development primarily as a device for fixing and intensifying our sympathy for Nanda. Such hesitation on the part of her lover would produce a combination of irony and poignancy that James found difficult to resist. This particular situation appeared in his work as early as *Daisy Miller.* But there is little evidence in the notebook entry, James's Preface, or the novel itself, that James means us to condemn Vanderbank, as we do Winterbourne, for his hesitancy. The contrary seems to have been James's intent, for in the Preface to *The Princess Casamassima,* he singled out Vanderbank for inclusion in his list of characters who functioned in his novels as "the most polished of possible mirrors of the subject." In this same passage, far from suggesting disapproval of Vanderbank's inaction, James indicates that it stems from "the vivacity in him, to his positive sorrow and loss, of the state of being aware."[9]

But long before either Preface or novel, in his account of the donnée of his story, James suggests an answer to the riddle of Vanderbank's hesitation, his failure to act even when urged by a genuine liking for Nanda, her evident love for him, and Mr. Longdon's cash. James underlines the intimacy which has existed between the young man and "the mother," whom he has "liked, visited, talked freely with, taken pleasure in." Now the actual treatment in the novel of the relationship between Van and Mrs. Brook has stimulated much speculation about an affair between the two, either in progress at the time, or terminated before the beginning of the story. The Duchess tells Longdon that Mrs. Brook wants Vanderbank "for herself," and although this may tantalize us it does not satisfy us as to the literal facts of the case. But surely we don't require such satisfaction. If James, at this early stage of his idea, was capable of using the term "horrors" when he meant, literally, risqué or even indecent talk; if he contemplated the exposure to such talk with the seriousness and emotion usu-

9. *Art of the Novel,* pp. 70-1.

ally reserved in the nineteenth century novel for the loss of virginity; if, finally, he could climax that exposure and certify the loss of "innocence" by having one of his characters produce a French novel as evidence; then surely we are to credit Van's past conversations with Mrs. Brook as invested with the emotional and evocative significance of an overtly sexual relation. We simply don't need the confirmation of specific details.

But this degree of intimacy with the mother means, quite logically for James, that the young man cannot take the daughter. He could conceivably "take her out of" her mother's influence, save her, that is, in the benevolent, sexually neutral fashion of Mr. Longdon at the end of the novel. However, he cannot simply take her, and the practical effect of Nanda's loss of ignorance is that she expects to be taken, as her mother was, not just saved. James appears to wish the reader to grasp and sympathize with Vanderbank's dilemma, although both the obscurity of treatment in the novel and our current notions of what is sexually sane make this difficult. We will return to Vanderbank later in our study of James's evocation of sexuality in Mrs. Brook. But there is one further point to be made before we leave our study of James's original conception of Vanderbank and the role he was to play in the novel. I am suggesting that James was not in the least disposed, as most critics of the novel are, to treat Vanderbank harshly in moral or psychological terms, as a case, for example, of paralysis of the will or the inability to feel after all of his analysis. As James saw it, Vanderbank simply could not marry the girl he might otherwise have chosen, and this was *because* Nanda has been exposed to a sexuality Van has enjoyed in his relations with Mrs. Brook. If this dilemma has a certain familiar ring, it is because it is similar in form to the one which James contrives for Nanda, a dilemma which Mitchy describes for Nanda herself in the following passage:

> "The man with '*the* kind' [of delicacy which would prevent him from loving a girl so exposed as Nanda] . . . happens to be just the type you *can* love? But what's the use," he persisted as she answered nothing, "in loving a person with the prejudice—hereditary or other—to which you're precisely obnoxious? Do you positively *like* to love in vain?"
>
> It was a question, the way she turned back to him seemed to say, that deserved a responsible answer. "Yes." [10]

There is no real evidence that James judged Vanderbank's dilemma perverse but found Nanda's pathetic. The author clearly believes that both are caught in insoluble contradiction, the result of

10. James, *The Awkward Age*, p. 359.

their inability to make awareness prevail over the force of sexual desire. They are both intended to be seen as victims, fine and subtle observers snared by passion. The design of this contradiction evokes sympathy for Nanda, but not for Vanderbank. Here James fails because, as with his final treatment of Hyacinth Robinson and Fleda Vetch, a design chosen for its beauty and rhetorical power simply affronts our stubborn sense of moral and psychological probability.

The notebook entry which we have been examining, like the novel itself, but unlike the Preface, presents us with the problem of the relationship between James's tone and the explicit content of his story. If we take *The Awkward Age* to be chiefly a study of the difficulties encountered when an outdated prejudice in favor of sexual ignorance in the young threatens the pleasure of uninhibited conversation, then the intense concern lavished on the whole affair would seem to be excessive. The conversations in Mrs. Brook's drawing room, though witty and often graceful, are neither brilliant nor shockingly indecent. And it must surely have occurred to James's contemporaries, not to speak of the modern reader, that the best way to engage our concern over the situation of innocence exposed was to expose it to something more than talk.

Nevertheless, the tone of the novel, particularly in key scenes dominated by Mrs. Brook, Nanda, or both, conveys unmistakably the sense of danger, waste, cruelty, and great sadness. (This of course is not to deny that in much of the novel, particularly the scenes in which the minor characters appear, the tone is much lighter.) Although James himself once described the treatment of his subject in *The Awkward Age* as "ironic—lightly and simply ironic!" few readers even moderately sympathetic to James have failed to catch a deeper resonance. Yvor Winters, though he also poses the most serious objections to the novel on other grounds, has described its effect upon him in this way:

> It is a remarkable evidence of the genius of James that though most of the important actions in the story are either flatly incredible or else are rendered so subtly as to be indeterminable, yet the resultant attitudes and states of mind of the actors are rendered with extraordinary poignancy: the obscure, slow, and ugly withdrawal of Vanderbank, the final scene between Mitchy and Nanda, the final departure of Nanda and Mr. Longdon . . . are, for myself, among the most haunting memories which I retain from my fragmentary experience as a reader of novels. Yet few memorable novels are less satisfactory.[11]

Given the seriousness and the intensity of tone exhibited in such

11. Winters, *Defense of Reason,* p. 322.

scenes, we find it impossible to content ourselves with the literal facts of the story. For example, Mrs. Brook's public revelation that Nanda has read an indecent novel, even after we have made full allowances for the mother's callousness, the daughter's chagrin, the suitor's discomfort, is not in itself a sufficient basis for the intense emotions generated by the act. Critics such as Maxwell Geismar seize on this apparent disproportion between literal fact and tone, and accuse James of a monstrous, obsessive sentimentality.

A way out of the dilemma sketched above, one usually taken by sympathetic critics, is unobtrusively to import into one's reading of *The Awkward Age* an emblematic interpretation of its literal details. Thus, in a typical interpretation of the novel as social portraiture, Mrs. Brook's revelation might become a vicious attack upon the freedom and integrity of her daughter (whereas James's contemporaries might well have read the scene as a calculated demonstration of her daughter's loss of virginity). Nanda, in our emblematic reading, is prevented, not just from entering a drawing room full of racy talk, but from openly adopting the sexual maturity and the intelligence that are hers by right. Vanderbank's delicacy becomes spiritual or psychological impotence. Lesser fry, such as Lord Petherton and Mr. Cashmore, begin to seem more sinister, menacing rather than trivial in their promiscuity. Longdon becomes the representative of older, more humane values and traditions, Nanda's protector after the episode of the French novel. The novel thus slips away from its own prosaic and trivial details and moves toward a "meaning" which is appropriate to its intense tone. It becomes a tragedy of an individual subjected to the corruptive force of a decadent society.

This type of reading, as I have indicated above, is not so much false to the novel as incomplete. Also, it has difficulty explaining such elements as the following: James's delight with the character of Mrs. Brook, a little too pronounced to be seen as merely aesthetic satisfaction in the creation of a character of whom the author disapproves; Vanderbank's inaction and Nanda's passivity, obscurity and non-resistance precisely where, if we assume the basic conflict is moral, there ought to be clarity and strength; the whole intricate system of contrasts, parallelism, and reversals by which James has woven together his characters in the novel. This last feature, though usually claimed as a technical device for the refinement of moral issues and conflict, is in fact so exuberantly displayed as to distract the reader from moral or social issues which, in this interpretation of the novel, the system is supposed to be serving.

Now all of these difficulties suggest the presence within the author of an interest amounting to fascination in some part of his subject. This fascination may coexist with the moral intention for a time, but it will eventually signal its presence and force by throwing into the moral conflict some such difficulty as those which I have described above. In looking for the source of James's interest in his subject, for an explanation of the intensity of tone which he makes emerge from trivial details, for an emblematic system that would enable me to take Nanda's French novel seriously, I return to James's portrayal of antagonistic forms of sexuality in mother and daughter. This interest was strong, non-moral at root, and pursued by the author with sufficient vigor and persistence to give to the novel its excitement and its intense tone. The interest was serious because it stemmed from one of James's most characteristic ways of responding to experience, not because it bespeaks a particularly deep insight into the nature of evil in late Victorian society. James's chief interest in *The Awkward Age* is the conflict generated by the polar opposition between the types of sexuality embodied in the characters of Mrs. Brook and Nanda.

If we press down at all insistently at any important point in the situation and action of the novel, we find ourselves dealing with the interplay of sexual forces. James talks a great deal in his Preface about various social systems devised for getting a girl into and through her mother's drawing room, but what becomes increasingly evident as we study Mrs. Brook's maneuvers, is that Nanda is her sexual competitor more importantly than she is an embarrassment to her drawing room. Let us not, as Mrs. Brook remarks to Mitchy, "be so awfully clever as to make it believed that we can never be simple." Nanda reveals her mother's age and thereby detracts from the power the older woman has exercised over the men in her salon. As James points out to us several times in the text, one of Mrs. Brook's own favorite poses is that of the ingénue, the charmingly bewildered woman beset by the cares of the world. With Nanda's emergence the mother is in danger of being upstaged, and the prospect is not a pleasant one.

The two women are in competition for Vanderbank. The scenes in which they make their appeals to him indicate fairly clearly the qualities which James associated with aggressive and passive sexuality. In Book Six, Mrs. Brook leads Vanderbank and Mitchy in what appears to be a sublimely detached and lucid analysis of Van's character, the kind of exercise on which the group prides itself and which they enter willingly, apparently having no need for the "excuse of passion." But Mrs. Brook at her most abstract is actually giving vent to strong, and for her, quite dangerous emotions. James clearly admires the sheer intuitive flights of her perception, as well as the masterful way in which she controls the two men's reactions. But this keenly intellectual capacity, shown to best advantage in this scene, is actually generated by, and put to the service of her fear that she is to lose Vanderbank to her daughter. Mrs. Brook fights with what she has and the rarefied quality of her weapons should not be allowed to obscure the source of her energy—which is fear and sexual jealousy.

Van has just blurted out to Mrs. Brook news of Mr. Longdon's offer to settle a large sum of money on Nanda if Van will marry her. The climax of Mrs. Brook's reaction is the following:

> "Why [I know that] so far as they count on you they count, my dear Van, on a blank." Holding him a minute as with the soft low voice of his fate, she sadly but firmly shook her head. "You won't do it." "Oh!" he almost too loudly protested. (295-96)

Mrs. Brook does not wish to lose him to Nanda; the Duchess is correct when she says that the mother wants him "for herself." But passion and the fear of sexual loss in Mrs. Brook translate themselves into a capacity for action and the manipulation of those around her. And, from James's point of view, it is an added distinction of Mrs. Brook's that the weapon by which she defends and promotes her desires is an almost affectedly detached rhetoric of analysis. In any event, she administers to Van what the ensnared and indecisive young man always requires from the sexually strong woman in James's fiction: "the soft low voice of his fate."

Nanda, on the other hand, offers to Van that which James found most moving in the situation of the sexually exposed innocent: a kind of nostalgia for the old ignorance, a wistful acceptance of her present fate, and an appeal to him to share her lot as aware of, but helpless before the way of the world. In the first passage which follows, Nanda speaks of Aggie in tones which foreshadow her eventual and most extravagant celebration of the ideal of passive sexuality: her arrangement of the disastrous, and by ordinary realistic standards, absurd marriage between Mitchy and Aggie.

> "Well," said Nanda with the frankest interest, "she's a miracle. If one could be her exactly, absolutely, without the least little mite of change, one would probably be wise to close with it." (343)

And here she makes her appeal, or rather she voices the appeal of her exposed state, to Vanderbank:

> "It's the tone and the current and the effect of all the others that push

you along," she went on as if she hadn't heard him. "If such things are contagious, as every one says, you prove it perhaps as much as any one. But you don't begin"—she continued blandly enough to work it out for him; "or you can't at least originally have begun. Any one would know that now—from the terrific effect I see I produce on you by talking this way. There it is—it's all out before one knows it, isn't it, and I can't help it any more than you can, can I?" So she appeared to put it to him, with something in her lucidity that would have been infinitely touching; a strange grave calm consciousness of their common doom and of what in especial in it would be worst for herself. (344)

The antagonistic forms of sexuality figured in the two women are thus displayed separately in scenes in which first Mrs. Brook, and then Nanda, confront Vanderbank, the object of their competition. In the climactic scene of the novel, which takes place in Book Eight, the two women are made to confront one another. The dramatic emphasis of the scene is placed squarely upon their respective sexual roles, and here, as throughout the novel, it is the conflict between sexual polarities, rather than social or moral criticism, which dominates James's own interest.

At this point in the novel Mitchy has acted, acceding to Nanda's desire that he marry her friend Aggie. Vanderbank, on the other hand, continues to temporize over Mr. Longdon's offer of a settlement should he propose to Nanda. The occasion for the scene is an evening party at Tishy Grendon's home, at which all the novel's major characters and the most important of the minor characters are present. The scene begins with Vanderbank's arrival at the Grendon home, where he is greeted by Nanda, who acts throughout this first part of the scene, precisely to the point of her mother's appearance, as hostess for the affair. Nanda has by now taken full command of the tangle of her friend's social and moral affairs, signifying to the reader that she has decisively passed down into the adult drawing room, and is indeed beginning to assert a kind of authority there.

The dramatization of this new power of Nanda's in her first few moments of conversation with Van reveals three facts of considerable importance to our understanding of the major themes of the novel. First, what is for James perhaps the most moving aspect of the plight of his innocents is that in their effort to achieve some form of maturity, they have only the model of their sexual rival to follow. Thus Nanda is here, as elsewhere in the novel, engaged in an unconscious imitation of her mother's social skill. The most prominent and disastrous consequence of such imitation on Nanda's part will turn out to be the marriage which she has arranged between Mitchy and Aggie, a mar-

riage which Nanda will persist in regarding as sublime in intention if
not in fact. Second, Nanda's temporary assumption of control of a
drawing room is a kind of halfway mark of her progress in the story.
It foreshadows the eventual development, in Book Ten, which sees
Nanda presiding over her mother's house while Mrs. Brook sits pa-
tiently or impatiently upstairs. (Here it is worth pointing out that this
later scene, although grossly incompatible with James's evocative picture of Nanda as the injured and frustrated innocent, dramatizes an
ironic reversal of roles between mother and daughter that is too
tempting for James to resist.) Third, we note from the opening of the
scene at Tishy Grendon's that there is no longer any real question of
Nanda's being passed swiftly through her mother's drawing room so
as to avoid the corruption of its talk. Rather, the problem which Mrs.
Brook must now face is that Nanda will not pass through at all, that
she will assume permanent control, or worse, that she will carry
off Vanderbank, Mrs. Brook's chief ornament. Subsequent events
show how aware Mrs. Brook is of the problem. Structurally, this first
exchange between Van and Nanda is intended to stand in utter contrast to the conclusion of the episode, at which Mrs. Brook drives
Nanda back into the submissiveness of a child.

Harold's arrival shifts the conversation to the possibility of
Nanda's being adopted by Mr. Longdon, an eventuality which Harold
counts on to keep him supplied with five-pound notes. In reply to
Tishy's question about what Nanda is doing at Mr. Longdon's house,
Harold displays some of the wit that has recently made him the fashion.

> "Why she's working Mr. Longdon, like a good true girl," Harold
> said; "like a good true daughter and even, though she doesn't love me
> nearly so much as I love *her*, I will say, like a good true sister. I'm
> bound to tell you, my dear Tishy," he went on, "that I think it awfully
> happy, with the trend of manners, for any really nice young thing to be
> a bit lost to sight. London, upon my honour, is quite too awful for
> girls, and any big house in the country is as much worse—with the
> promiscuities and opportunities and all that—as you know for your-
> selves." (391-92)

As subsequent incidents in the scene demonstrate, there are a
variety of ways in which these people "work" one another, and the
whole scene, we should note in anticipation, is an excellent example of
the manner in which James works the reader in the novel as a whole.
His chief effect will be to suspend us between admiration for the sheer
energy of Mrs. Brook, as she seeks to dislodge a potentially challeng-
ing rival, and our reflexive dismay at the situation of that rival, Mrs.
Brook's daughter. And if it is not true to say that Nanda herself is

working Mr. Longdon, we may still claim that the condition represented in the girl exercises a very strong affective force upon him, as
it did upon James himself, and as the author intends it to operate on
the reader when, in Book Ten, Nanda finally breaks into tears before
Mr. Longdon. Harold, meanwhile, is beginning to occupy something
of the same position held by Lord Petherton in the circle. Like
Petherton, he's the amiable predator on the outskirts of the group
whose exploits provide the more cerebral members with materials for
analysis.

A large part of the scene at Tishy Grendon's is given over to a
conversation—actually a monologue with anxious replies—between
the Duchess and Mr. Longdon. The Duchess lays siege to the older
man in an effort to persuade him to redouble his efforts to secure
Vanderbank as Nanda's husband. In this the Duchess's motives are
predictable at the beginning of the conversation and perfectly clear
when, at the end of the scene, we are given to understand that Lord
Petherton and Aggie are having an affair. The Duchess and Mrs.
Brook, the two women in whom both an aggressive sexuality and a
superb social skill are displayed, compete with one another throughout, their verbal exchanges providing much of the book's pointed
humor. The particular basis of competition at this point, and the
reason for the Duchess's fervent desire to see Van married off at once,
is that she herself has suffered the fate which Mrs. Brook is trying to
avoid: the Duchess has been supplanted by a sexual rival, her
daughter. She is eager to see the same happen to Mrs. Brook. Of course
the Duchess, like Mrs. Brook later in the scene, professes no other
motive than that of seeing the friend of her own child comfortably
married, a bit of piety which reveals the manner in which James has
contrived a neatly balanced dilemma for both mothers and daughters in
the sexual game. Nanda embodies the desire for a maturity which has
no model in her environment other than her mother's talent for manipulation. The mothers, on the other hand, are checked in their
desire for power and sexual freedom by the code of maternal love, a
code to which they are compelled to defer even as it provides protection for a rival. The attack by the Duchess upon Mrs. Brook as
"dangerous" is paralleled structurally at the end of the scene as Mrs.
Brook delightedly speculates about what has happened to her friend's
lover.

The conversation between the Duchess and Mr. Longdon is inter-
rupted by Mrs. Brook's approach as she begins her assault on the by
now clearly frightened Longdon. Vanderbank is at her side, and the

motive which animates Mrs. Brook throughout the remainder of the
scene is of course that he should remain there. At first the talk is
casual, the theme being the deterioration of the circle since Mitchy's
marriage. Mrs. Brook then begins her strategy.

> "Oh you're out of step, Duchess," Vanderbank said. "We used all to
> march abreast, but we're falling to pieces. It's all, saving your presence,
> Mitchy's marriage."
> "Ah," Mrs. Brook concurred, "how thoroughly I feel that! Oh, I
> knew. The spell's broken; the harp has lost a string. We're not the same
> thing. *He's* not the same thing."
> "Frankly, my dear," the Duchess answered, "I don't think that you
> personally are either."
> "Oh, as for that—which is what matters least—we shall perhaps
> see." With which Mrs. Brook turned again to Mr. Longdon. "I haven't
> explained to you what I meant just now. We want Nanda." (416-17)

Mrs. Brook clearly does not want Nanda. Rather, secure by this
time in her belief that not even Longdon's money will induce Van to
propose, Mrs. Brook wants to jostle Longdon into declaring himself
and adopting Nanda. When this particular strategy breaks on the rock
of her husband's dullness, Mrs. Brook brilliantly modifies her plan. She
stages a scene of scandal for Mr. Longdon, an incidental virtue of
which is that it allows her to humiliate the Duchess, and thereby ensures that Nanda will eventually be removed from such a corrupt
atmosphere. The whole scene ends with Mrs. Brook triumphant in her
favorite role of the ingénue, expressing horror at the discovery that
Nanda has read a shocking French novel.

What James's own strategy in this scene and in the whole novel
reveals is a fascination with conflicting sexual roles far deeper and
artistically much more significant than any commitment to social re-
form or moral outrage. He was powerfully moved, in quite different
ways, by both the younger and the older woman, by both the sexually
mature and aggressive and the innocent. What we get in *The Awkward Age* is a kind of artistic preliminary exercise in the evocative
power of the theme of sexual conflict. Later James will exploit the
theme for much more serious reasons. He will make use of it, in fact,
as a device for the celebration of those intensely individual qualities to
which he *was* most committed. This happens in *The Wings of the
Dove*.

6

THE WINGS OF THE DOVE

The Wings of the Dove is James's most ambitious novel and the richest product of his fascination with the design of polar opposition. In terms of this design James conceived of his heroine, plotted her movement from the beginning to the end of the novel, and celebrated what were for him primary human values. The novel is long, complex in its relationships, and sometimes very dense in its prose; for the sake of clarity, and to indicate the points at which I depart from majority opinion on the novel, I will briefly summarize my sense of the importance of the design as fixed in Milly Theale's character, the action, and the view of experience which that action is meant to celebrate.

James first speaks in his notebook of the character who is to become Milly Theale in terms which recall the first appearance of Isabel Archer.

> Isn't perhaps something to be made of the idea that came to me some time ago and that I have not hitherto made any note of—the little idea of the situation of some young creature (it seems to me preferably a woman, but of this I'm not sure), who, at 20, on the threshold of a life that has seemed boundless, is suddenly condemned to death (by consumption, heart-disease, or whatever) by the voice of the physician?[1]

1. *The Notebooks*, p. 169.

"On the threshold of a life that has seemed boundless" and "condemned to death" are the polarities which pressed upon James's imagination with an insistence equal to that of the idea of the "poor girl, who has dreamed of freedom," and who finds herself "ground in the very mill of the conventional." Minny Temple was of course the prototype for both fictional young women. What I wish to stress at this point is that the conception of this most radical of all of James's polarities, limitless possibility for life and certain death, is not just the starting point for Milly Theale but rather the dominant note of her characterization throughout the novel. We misunderstand and underestimate the force of what James is trying to do in the book if we assume, as some critics do, that Milly's imminent death is a device for making more poignant her betrayal, more vicious the acts of the betrayers. On the contrary, I will argue that the whole mechanism of Kate Croy's plot, as richly and interestingly developed as it is, is primarily meant to subserve the chief task which James has set for himself, that of giving particular, and intense, and therefore heroic form to what would otherwise be a diffuse and hopelessly generalized desire "to live." Kate Croy's plot is one of the ways in which James saves Milly from an obscure or fragmented intensity, just as Madame Merle's plot rescued Isabel from the endless exercise of negative freedom, or on the other hand, a truly autonomous and hence more seriously compromising choice. In both novels the immediate effect of what we call evil is an aesthetic one: it gives, from outside the heroine, precision and clarity, an intelligibility, to what had previously been the vague desire to be free and to live.

However much we may be intrigued by the mechanics or the agents of deception we must not lose sight of the design of polarity which *chiefly* animates and explains the treatment of both Isabel and Milly Theale. Only by focusing our attention on the design worked out in *The Portrait of a Lady* could we avoid endless speculation about Isabel's personal or conscious motivation. Similarly, to lose sight of the enduring importance in *The Wings of the Dove* of the conflict between generalized desire to live and imminent death is to resign Milly to the status of passive victim and cede the novel to Kate Croy. But this, as I hope to demonstrate, is to make nonsense or disposable piety out of the last book of the novel, the section in which Milly, although victim to be sure, becomes quite intensely active. Although the modern critic is likely to experience some misgivings over the implications of this final book, we must try to grasp the ending in James's terms. This means close attention throughout to the workings of the extreme conflict centered in Milly Theale, the conflict which explains her initial appearance and James's fascination with her.

Milly's literal movement in the novel is from life to death; the burden of James's treatment imposes upon her story quite the opposite movement. Nothing can be done about the literal fact; there is obviously no room in Milly's case, as there is in Isabel's, for speculation about whether she will escape, or what form this escape will take. Milly dies, but only after she has been manipulated through an action and by means of a technique designed to persuade us that at the point of her death she is more vital than at any other point in the novel, that her progress through the novel has been away from death toward life, whatever the literal facts of the case may be. Even at the time of his second notebook entry James has his hand upon this design, and expresses it in this way:

> I seem to get hold of the tail of a pretty idea in making that happiness, that life, that snatched experience the girl longs for, BE, *in fact,* some rapturous act of that sort — some act of generosity, of passionate beneficence, of pure sacrifice, to the man she loves.[2]

It may seem that even at this early stage of analysis I have entangled my argument in contradiction, for thus far I have described a heroine conceived to embody the possibility of life and the certainty of death. On the other hand, I have described the action of the novel as a movement between these two poles which affirms what is denied by the literal facts concerning the heroine. The contradiction is only apparent, for the movement in the novel takes Milly to an act, and a spiritual condition which in James's own mind both transcended and transformed concrete facts of life and death, as well as the social and moral values over which they preside. The novel is not tragic; it rather advances a view of experience which is religious and transcendent.

Milly lives at the end, as James explicitly notes, not only through the act of sacrifice to Densher with which she gives up her life, but also, and rather disconcertingly for the critic of the novel, she lives in the devastating power she wields in the last book of the novel. Since she is removed from the scene entirely, we may claim that the effects of her sacrifice upon Densher and Kate are quite beyond Milly's intent or control, accidents if we wish. Or we may say that in the light of the deception practiced on her by the English pair, Kate and Densher get what they deserve according to poetic justice or some other secular

2. *Ibid.,* pp. 171-72.

morality. But whereas Milly may be absent, James is clearly not. He deals neither in accidents nor, I hope to demonstrate, in the allocation of rewards and punishments in accordance with moral schemes sanctioned merely by reason or social values. Kate's note at the end is not what we should call penitent; nor does she remark the functioning of some nicely calibrated moral machine. She speaks rather of radical, qualitative change, the product of a transcendent power, and the chief effect of that vitality toward which Milly moves as she moves toward her literal death. Kate simply says, "We shall never be again as we were."

Of course it is the quality of experience represented by the character and actions of Milly Theale that James wishes to celebrate in *The Wings of the Dove*. As with all of James's major figures we understand the general form of this experience and its accompanying emotion more clearly than we understand its substance. We are to be moved by Milly's desire to live and to experience love, and questions about specific details of that love just do not arise. No one asks with any seriousness or persistence why it is that Milly loves and wishes to be loved by this particular individual, Merton Densher. James is successful here, as he was not with Fleda Vetch and Nanda Brookenham, in persuading the reader to accept and be moved by a generalized passion without enquiring too deeply into the psychological origins or implications of that passion. Imminent death and the urgency it inspires afford James the partial release from plausibility his art required.

Milly's desire is accorded a high value by the author because by its nature and all of James's art it cannot be satisfied in the ordinary ways in which heroines are satisfied. Again, this is a matter not of Milly's personal psychology but rather of James's overall use of her within the novel. Supposing that we could somehow eliminate tuberculosis, Kate Croy, and Densher's hesitation, still no one could possibly expect Milly's desire to be conventionally satisfied once James has introduced her sitting on a rock contemplating the kingdoms of the earth. She will fall or she will be pushed, but she isn't going to be satisfied with a piece of a kingdom we could measure in the specific social or moral terms of the realistic novel.

Finally, the experience rendered through Milly Theale is valued by James insofar as it both escapes and defeats what James saw as the inevitable corruption of ordinary desire. Thus Milly's life *is* the sacrifice which she makes at the point of death and by that sacrifice she transforms and devastates the moral and social landscape she is leaving. Here, as we shall see, the ideal for which Fleda Vetch struggled so fiercely gets its final vindication and celebration.

Desire in which the form and the intensity is more important than the object desired; which can be satisfied, if at all, only in some transcendent fashion; which displays itself best in victory over the ordinary or the corrupt—this is the type of experience celebrated by Milly Theale', story, and it should be fairly obvious, instrumental to that celebration is the opposition between Milly and Kate Croy. A point that is perhaps not so obvious, and one which I want to examine in my analysis, is the manner in which this particular design is developed in terms of James's treatment of the theme of sexuality in his two young women. But first we must consider more thoroughly James's placement of his polar design in the central character of the novel.

In the Preface to *The Wings of the Dove,* James described the major problem he faced in his treatment of Milly Theale, given her essential fictive identity as a young woman "on the threshold of life," but "condemned to death." The interest in such a character necessarily lay not in her abjectly submitting to the processes of death but rather in the vitality with which she affronts that destiny. The certainty of death must be made to sharpen and intensify her effort to live. Milly is made to agree with James on this score, so that an important part of the novel's realistic treatment of Milly is her strenuous effort to conceal her illness, to avoid "smelling of the sickroom."

But, if he was unwilling to allow his heroine to express directly the panic or despair of the dying, James still does not wish to forgo the elemental, powerfully evocative effect of his heroine's situation. His solution was to treat these fixed contraries of Milly's situation by means of the novel's imagery, and through the choric, celebratory role of Susan Stringham. The third strategy by which he hoped to achieve pathos without wholly abandoning his heroine to it, was to dramatize at considerable length Milly's effort to learn whether or not her disease is incurable. Thus, James exploits the affective power of a fixed and hence pathetic destiny while dramatizing the energy with which his heroine seeks to discover and accept that destiny. Milly's long conversations with Sir Luke Strett and her reflections on these conversations are very far removed from factual exchange between doctor and patient, are indeed darkened with the atmosphere of the hunt, and sometimes even obscured by the subtlety of both pursuer and pursued. This is not complexity for its own sake, although the density of these passages and the heavy aura of mystery surrounding the simple facts about Milly's illness have irritated many readers. The density is simply the charged medium through which Milly tries to expand her consciousness of reality, and through this most typical of all Jamesian struggles resists the death fixed in James's very conception of her role in the novel.

The imagery in the novel is, as I have said, the chief technical means by which James focused his design, insofar as it was incorporated in the person of Milly Theale. Extensively analyzed by critics of the novel, this imagery gives poetic expression to the conjoined and balanced elements of vitality and death in Milly's character. "Poetic" is used with some hesitation, since the term has often been casually evoked to describe the novel and is in any case difficult to control. I mean here the conscious use of an extended image to interrupt the novel's characteristic preoccupation with what is specific, contingent, and local, and make us perceive in the heroine's experience a general and invariable condition of human life. This is what James is trying to do with Milly in the novel as a whole, and this is the effect of such a passage as the following:

> Once more things melted together—the beauty and the history and the facility and the splendid midsummer glow: it was a sort of magnificent maximum, the pink dawn of an apotheosis coming so curiously soon. What in fact befell was that, as she afterwards made out, it was Lord Mark who said nothing in particular—it was she herself who said all. She couldn't help that—it came; and the reason it came was that she found herself, for the first moment, looking at the mysterious portrait through tears. Perhaps it was her tears that made it just then so strange and fair—as wonderful as he had said: the face of a young woman, all splendidly drawn, down to the hands, and splendidly dressed; a face almost livid in hue, yet handsome in sadness and crowned with a mass of hair, rolled back and high, that must, before fading with time, have had a family resemblance to her own. The lady in question, at all events, with her slightly Michael-angelesque squareness, her eyes of other days, her full lips, her long neck, her recorded jewels, her brocaded and wasted reds, was a very great personage—only unaccompanied by a joy. And she was dead, dead, dead. Milly recognized her exactly in words that had nothing to do with her. "I shall never be better than this." [3]

The passage is richly detailed; the scene forms a part of the dramatic intercourse between Lord Mark and Milly at a particular point in time; and, quite pointedly, James constructs his picture of the Bronzino through Milly's consciousness, as she later recalls the scene. Detail, relationship, retrospection, all are characteristic features of the

3. James, *The Wings of the Dove,* I, pp. 220-221.

novel, the Jamesian novel. But the image is poetic, and we may legitimately use the term here because all of the details point beyond sensation to the conjunction of life, with all that this entails at its richest, and death. Lord Mark as an actor in a novelistic scene has been left behind, as his remark to Milly makes clear. ("He hadn't understood.") And finally, although we get the whole image through Milly's consciousness, that very consciousness is subtly released here from the exigencies and the probabilities of this particular woman's situation. Most obviously indicative of this is the construction of the passage with its rhetorical climax in "and she was dead, dead, dead," to which Milly's spoken reaction is the lovely and impersonal "I shall never be better than this." Literally, what happens here is that Milly Theale looks at a painting of a beautiful and rich young woman, whose life and wealth have been caught in art after her death. Milly thinks of her own life. She thinks *through* the obvious reference to her own illness, and thereby arrives at a kind of joy, partly aesthetic, partly mystical, over a fact of experience which, in its particular application to individual men, is most feared. She sees the fusion of life and death poetically, and that is the manner in which we are supposed to see her in the scene. This type of image freezes the action and the other elements of the dramatic scene into something approaching a tableau, the figures of which momentarily become poetic emblems rather than fictional characters. Another example of such an effect occurs later in this same Book Five of the novel when Milly walks in the park after her interview with Sir Luke.

A second type of image used to heighten the design which animates Milly Theale is the figure of speech by which the other characters try to describe her or their reactions to her. I have in mind, of course, the image of the dove which Kate Croy first applies to her. So much has been written about James's employment of this figure that I need only add one or two points. This type of image, as J. A. Ward has pointed out, is much more a function of the dramatic action of the novel and the development of its relationships than the one I have analyzed above. As he shows, the use of the image is itself a part of Kate's strategy, that of fashioning and imposing on Milly the type of role most convenient to her plan.[4] Milly accepts this role, though doubtful of the truth of the image, because of the urgency of her desire for life.

The image is also an index to the state of the relationship between

4. Ward, *The Search*, p. 180-96. For a more extended discussion of the image of the dove, see Matthiessen, *James*, pp. 68-72.

Milly and Kate, the dove figure used by Kate to refer to Milly's vulnerability, her wealth and beauty, and finally to the power which she exercises at the end of the book. I want here to add only what is perhaps
obvious, but nevertheless of basic importance in James's manipulation
of the image. It fuses for us and holds in our minds the association of
beauty and fragility at the very heart of the author's conception of
Milly, a beauty which exists *because* of its fragility. Similarly, the bib-
lical references which the image evokes convey the paradoxical idea
of power achieved because of, and through death. The image is thus
perfectly accurate to James's sense of the polar design embodied in
Milly, and this remains true whatever other complexities may have
been spun by author, the characters, or the critics.

A third type of imagery used to subserve James's design is more
overtly poetic and at the same time more clearly normative. James
intervenes directly as narrator to underline for the reader the terms
of Milly's situation, and to focus on her determination to avoid show-
ing any sign of her illness. The following passage is a good example
of the type of image I have in mind. It is not common in the novel,
but very important to the working out of the dilemma which James
foresaw in his Preface: how to evoke the pathos of imminent and certain death, without at the same time relinquishing his heroine to passivity. Here, the heroine's very stillness is made to appear superior
to, and more vital than the restless energy with which Kate Croy moves
throughout the novel, acting in a manner and in spheres which James's
conception of Milly will not allow her to do.

> Certain aspects of the connexion of these young women show for us,
> such is the twilight that gathers about them, in the likeness of some dim
> scene in a Maeterlinck play; we have positively the image, in the delicate
> dusk, of the figures so associated and yet so opposed, so mutually
> watchful: that of the angular pale princess, ostrich-plumed, black robed,
> hung about with amulets, reminders, relics, mainly seated, mainly still,
> and that of the upright restless slow-circling lady of her court who
> exchanges with her, across the black water streaked with evening gleams,
> fitful questions and answers. The upright lady, with thick dark braids
> down her back, drawing over the grass a more embroidered train, makes
> the whole circuit, and makes it again, and the broken talk, brief and spar-
> ingly allusive, seems more to cover than to free their sense. (II, 139-40)

For all of her energy and her capacity for action, it is Kate who
here watches and admires the struggle in which, for all her surface
calm, Milly is deeply engaged. What Milly guards, literally, is her
composure under the knowledge that her disease is incurable, so that
the fantastic and utterly stationary figure in the image becomes, in

spite of the physical motion of the dark haired, "upright lady," the source of a superior vitality. Her fight to repress emotion is, by the logic of James's image, accorded a value appropriate to heroic action.

[Kate] . . . easily saw that for the girl to be explicit was to betray divinations, gratitudes, glimpses of the felt contrast between her fortune and her fear — all of which would have contradicted her systematic bravado. That was it, Kate wonderingly saw: to recognize was to bring down the avalanche — the avalanche Milly lived so in watch for and that might be started by the lightest of breaths; though less possibly the breath of her own stifled plaint than that of the vain sympathy, the mere helpless gaping inference of others. (II, 140-41)

Related to his use of imagery in support of the design of Milly's character in the novel is James's treatment of his international theme. For the working out of this familiar theme seems to me to be, more clearly perhaps than in his other novels, a function of James's primary interest in evocative polar design. Milly is American and rich. By the cultural convention of the day, to which James gave extensive elaboration, she is entitled to make a claim on life and Europe unthought of by her European counterpart. This being the case, James gains a sharply ironic effect from the disparity between what Milly has a virtual right to expect, that right staked out earlier by Daisy Miller and Isabel Archer, and that which actually is ahead of her.

But the irony and the paradox lay somewhat deeper than this, for in the novel James amplifies and gives resonance to his design in Milly by exploiting a perception of the character of American life to be found in his work as early as *Roderick Hudson*. Milly's story gives blunt expression to the theme to which not only American characters but American writers have paid repeated tribute: this is the concept of the American as being, uniquely, the man who can live intensely but only on the condition that he burn himself out quickly while doing so. With Milly Theale, James evokes the theme and tries to find a way out of the dilemma that is posed in some form or another by American heroes from Ishmael to Jake Barnes, and by writers from Poe to Fitzgerald: the fear that the quality of experience depends on its proximity to death, and that an experience not terminated by death will suffer a worse decay in time. Milly Theale is another version of the American in a desperate hurry, whose desperation is thought to be the source of his creativity and his strength.

One of the roles assigned Susan Stringham in the novel is that of sustaining in the mind of the reader this distinctly national quality of the contradictory forces invested in Milly's character. For example,

James uses her point of view to tell us that although Milly has come
to Europe to live and be entertained as the heiress of the ages, she
leaves behind her the wreckage of her former life. That is, like so
many other Americans of her century, the amplitude of her desire
seems directly proportionate to the chaos she has left behind:

> It was New York mourning, it was New York hair, it was a New York
> history, confused as yet, but multitudinous, of the loss of parents,
> brothers, sisters, almost every human appendage, all on a scale and with
> a sweep that had required the greater stage; it was a New York legend
> of affecting, of romantic isolation, and, beyond everything, it was by
> most accounts, in respect to the mass of money so piled on the girl's
> back, a set of New York possibilities. (I, 105-06)

Mrs. Stringham first identifies Milly Theale as a princess, but
suffers occasional vague anxiety that this "potential heiress of all the
ages" may be in some mysterious fashion subject to inexplicable
passion or impulse, that Milly may in the end treat her to "one of
the finer, one of the finest, one of the rarest . . . cases of American
intensity." All of which speculation is heady stuff for Susan, the
literary lady from Burlington, Vermont, "which she boldly upheld as
the real heart of New England, Boston being 'too far south.' "

It is also amusing for the reader, who perceives in Mrs. Stringham
the note of other middle-aged romantics who have traveled with, or
discovered in Europe, a young American who is to be the means of
securing, vicariously, a second chance at life. If in her more achingly
romantic moments Mrs. Stringham leans toward Catherine Sloper's
Aunt Penniman—for Mrs. Stringham discovers in herself a romantic
attachment to Merton Densher—she is still capable of reminding us
of Strether. She begs Densher to lie to Milly at the end of the novel,
just as Strether advises Chad to remain with Madame de Vionnet. Both
actions, drastic departures from the morality of Burlington and
Woolett, both about equally naive, are made to seem admirable.

Mrs. Stringham is a technical device, the Jamesian confidante;
she is also a comic portrait of the provincial American, her exalted
sentiment recognizable as twin to Henrietta Stackpole's blunt literal-
ism in its preference for theory over the facts of experience; also, in
somewhat the same way in which he uses Henrietta, James makes use
of Susan to protect his heroine. We are not disposed to regard Milly's
error as foolish when our attention is deflected to a much more obvious
case of romantic naiveté. But in addition to these uses, and in the
very first book in which she appears, Susan Stringham, through the
medium of her fancy, helps to identify as peculiarly American the

dilemma posed by Milly's character. This is not to say that Susan is herself fully conscious of the significance of her imaginative flights, and the reader, encouraged to take her comically, is apt to miss some of their full significance.

A case in point is the well-known scene in Book Three in which Susan leaves their mountain hotel to go in search of Milly, who has set out on a walk on the mountain. Susan comes upon the girl seated on a rock and gazing down at the valley below. What is always emphasized about the scene is the mythic or fairy-tale-like grandeur associated with Milly, her apparent power and the rather impersonal self-confidence with which she seems to survey the whole world for what it can offer her. Susan is exalted by this idea. Although neither young nor rich, she is American also, and so she finds nothing incongruous in such grand expectation. But what has been insufficiently noticed in discussions of the scene is the immediate association in Susan's mind between grand desire and death, not death alone, but suicide.

> For Mrs. Stringham stifled a cry on taking in what she believed to be the danger of such a perch for a mere maiden; her liability to slip, to slide, to leap, to be precipitated by a single false movement, by a turn of the head—how could one tell?—into whatever was beneath. . . . What had first been offered [Mrs. Stringham] was the possibility of a latent intention—however wild the idea—in such a posture; of some betrayed accordance of Milly's caprice with a horrible hidden obsession. (I, 123-24)

Moments afterwards Susan drives the thought from her mind, concludes that "the future wasn't to exist for her princess in the form of any sharp or simple release from the human predicament." It will instead "be a question of taking full in the face the whole assault of life." (I, 125)

> [Milly] wouldn't have committed suicide; she knew herself unmistakably reserved for some more complicated passage; this was the very vision in which she had, with no little awe, been discovered. The image that thus remained with the elder lady kept the character of a revelation. (I, 125)

James's intent would seem to be clear enough here: to signal through Susan's consciousness that however intense and painful Milly Theale's dilemma is to become she is not to be afforded the escape provided by melodramatic violence. She will take life's assault "full in the face." But without being perverse or overly ingenious, I think we can discover here something of what we have seen to be James's

characteristic practice of exploiting the affective powers of melodrama without tying himself to the simplicities of its literal action.

For the essence of James's conception of Milly in the novel is
that she will live most intensely as she draws closer to death. We speak
now not of motive or conscious intent, but of what Milly is made to
do and be by the novel's total effect, by the cumulative force of its action and technique. There is clearly no question of her escaping either
the physical death that awaits her, or the betrayal arranged by Kate
Croy and James. James, as we saw, was most explicit in his notebook
entry that Milly is to live most beautifully in an action taken on the
point of death. Given these facts, facts which make Milly Theale more
the embodiment of the Jamesian design than a character who owes her
identity to specific moral or psychological traits, it does not seem too
unlikely that we are meant to retain a kind of residual emotion from
Susan's first fear, even long after we have laid away the possibility of
literal suicide. We reflect that in the scene we have just considered,
Milly is pictured sitting upon a rock looking down "on the kingdoms
of the earth," apparently hers to take as the American princess. The
leap which Mrs. Stringham momentarily fears would be not away
from, but down into these kingdoms. James's plan for Milly, predicated
on his initial conception of her, and massively, minutely advanced by
the whole novel, seems to me to be precisely this: the story of a young
woman condemned to death but with the energy to plunge into it
rather than suffer it passively. The heroism of such a plunge is meant to
arise out of the sacrifice and death it entails.

Milly's specific acts in the novel, as well as the imagery and the
commentary of other characters, reflect the design incorporated in
her character. J.A. Ward recognizes the quality of her energy in "the
aggressiveness," fed by desperation, by which she plunges into the
experience of London.[5] What we have here is the assertiveness of the
American, cultural product of a radical Protestant individualism and
intriguing phantasies of endless frontiers, spiritualized, justified, and
made heroic by the specific impasse which constitutes Milly's character. She is in London, but her situation places her spiritually on the
outer reaches of experience where movement, plunge, and intensity
are all that count.

After Book Five, James depicts Milly's energy largely in terms
of its affective force in Densher's life. But for an extended period in
Books Four and Five, we see directly through Milly's consciousness
something of the excitement and the assurance with which she involves

5. Ward, *The Search*, p. 194.

herself in the life of Lancaster Gate. Her reactions at the dinner party given by Maud Lowder on her arrival in London show how successfully James could render directly Milly's intense desire and capacity for experience when he chose to do so:

> She thrilled, she consciously flushed, and all to turn pale again, with the certitude—it had never been so present—that she should find herself completely involved: the very air of the place, the pitch of the occasion, had for her both so sharp a ring and so deep an undertone. The smallest things, the faces, the hands, the jewels of the women, the sound of words, especially of names, across the table. the shape of the forks, the arrangement of the flowers, the attitude of the servants, the walls of the room, were all touches in a picture and denotements in a play; and they marked for her moreover her alertness of vision. She had never, she might well believe, been in such a state of vibration. . . . (I, 148)

In retrospect we mark the signs in such a passage of Milly's vulnerability: her delight with, and efforts to stimulate intense emotion in herself; the provincial fascination for the glamorous bits and pieces of English culture, "especially . . . names," the tendency to make herself a spectator, her experience a play. But the simple, strong desire for experience which such a passage conveys crucially involves Milly herself, the actual and here realistically rendered young woman, in the same design which emerges from the imagery, the manipulation of subordinate characters, and James's use of his international theme. Milly herself acts out, through the vivid play of her emotions in this conversation with Lord Mark, the terms of the design she serves in the novel. Her final remark to him, the climax of her excitement and the triumphant assertion of that quality which is to render her so comparatively easy a victim, comes in this passage:

> "You're *blasé*, but you're not enlightened. You're familiar with everything, but conscious really of nothing. What I mean is that you've no imagination." (I, 162)

Milly wishes to make the most of the opportunity for life afforded by English society and opened up for the first time at this gathering. She experiences the event with a vivacity far exceeding anything of which the other characters are capable. Through this very vivacity, this imaginative plunge, she moves herself materially closer to the betrayal that Kate Croy will eventually effect. This bit of action, dealing directly with Milly and devised to render dramatically the contradiction she embodies, has its counterpart in Book Five of the novel. Here, Milly's intelligence and that almost painfully sharp awareness that James always gives his heroines are again displayed as she fights her way through Sir Luke's delicacy to the truth that she is going to die.

Thus, throughout the novel Milly Theale exists with perfect consistency as the embodiment of the design with which James first began to speculate about the novel: she is the young woman on the threshold of life but condemned to death. James avoids making her the purely passive recipient of such a destiny by releasing her, through his imagery, from the confines of realism, and investing her condition with a poetic, that is general and deeply affective meaning for the reader. Susan Stringham is used to celebrate the American princess and underline implicitly the cultural significance of the design of intense life linked only to death. Finally, those scenes in which Milly's thoughts and feelings are made simultaneously to reflect a capacity for life, and a liability for betrayal and death, give dramatic expression to the design insofar as it is focused in her person.

Both Isabel Archer and Milly Theale are victimized, by women and strategies which bear some resemblance to one another. Madame Merle, after many years of trying to adjust her social pretensions to her meagre income, arranges Isabel's marriage to a former lover so that her daughter might profit from Isabel's fortune. Kate of course tries to secure a fortune for herself by sacrificing her lover for the short time Milly has left to live. Kate thereby hopes to achieve independence from her Aunt Maud Lowder, who will otherwise impose upon her life a social and personal tyranny comparable to that experienced less personally by Madame Merle in her career as the perfect guest. Both women, in planning their deception, are shrewd enough to realize that their best hope lies not in direct manipulation of the innocent, but rather in a tactful reliance upon Isabel's desire to be free, and Milly's to live. Isabel's desire is so intense and at the same time so extravagant as to require, for James, resolution in the choice of a man who embodies the opposite of freedom. Similarly, Kate realizes that Milly's desire to experience is so urgent under the certitude of death that she will go to considerable lengths—as she does—to ignore the real possibility that Merton Densher loves, and will continue to love another woman.

And yet it is precisely at this point, where we begin to focus upon the spectacular errors of the two heroines, that we have begun forcibly to extricate ourselves from the design and the rhetorical effects of the Jamesian action. Here, we approach questions of personal psychology which were not meant to be pursued. We may, if we

wish, ask why it is that Milly Theale persists in the belief that Densher
will return her love, even after considerable indication that this is unlikely, and we can even supply possible answers to this question. But
surely such a response to the character is similar to that which mis-
leads us into speculation about Isabel's precise motivation for ignoring
the advice of her friends. For the reader is to regard the choice of, on
the one hand, a sterile aesthete, and on the other, a man already engaged, as appropriate not so much to the psychology of either woman
as to that intensely abstract desire which is incorporated in them both:
respectively, the desire to be free and the desire to experience love. The
relevant question is not "Why do Isabel and Milly choose as they do?"
It is rather "What possible resolution could James devise for a desire
which is at once so extravagant and so urgent?"

The answer was a disappointment so crushing, so absurdly and
pathetically opposed to the original desire as to validate it, to give it
the kind of substantial reality and beauty which this desire lacked.
The answer supplied by Osmond and Kate Croy's Densher, by the
very thoroughness with which it negates the expectations of the
heroines, is a satisfactory dramatic resolution, probably the only possible one in a novelistic world, to their initial desire. Betrayal and deception bring down Isabel Archer and Milly Theale. But much more
importantly, such evil gives a substance and an affective force to that
intense but hitherto vague desire which the Jamesian heroine embodies. If we can never be precisely certain what such desire might
have come to without the intervention of Kate and Madame Merle,
we still concede it a substantial reality once it is locked into conflict
with the very specific and concretely intelligible plans of those who
betray and exploit. The blunt facts of betrayal save the Jamesian
heroine from the rarefied atmosphere of her own desire.

But first of all, the character Kate Croy is designed and used
by James to rescue Milly Theale from the impersonal fate which was
Minny Temple's, that of dying young when her intelligence, social
position, and courage might have allowed her to accomplish much.
Such a fate is common, but so far as the Jamesian heroine is concerned, it would be degrading. It does not substantiate and validate
the heroine's vague ambition by means of direct polar opposition; it
merely makes ambition irrelevant, at best the pathetic gesture of a
human being denied the dignity of personal opposition and reduced by
the commonplace facts of illness and death. This is why, once James
has thoroughly exploited his conception of the design figured in Milly
Theale, the image of her on the threshold of life and condemned to

death, he must turn the focus of his tale upon Kate's strategy. Kate will validate Milly's desire, whereas the death which Minny Temple suffered would merely cancel it. As we have seen, Milly's heroism is displayed in the imagery which James constructs and moderates for her; it is exhibited in the direct dramatic representation of the energy with which the young woman throws herself into the life of Lancaster Square, the only sphere available to her, and in the courage with which she pursues the truth in her relations with Sir Luke. This is as far as Milly, the unaided heroine, can go in support of the novel's intention: that of offering a desire to live which is sufficiently strong to provide a counterforce to the fact of death.

The rest is up to Kate Croy. The strategy devised by her in the novel is the means by which James arranges an opposition for Milly Theale proportionate to the value established in her character. Milly's imminent death is a suitable device for achieving pathos; Kate's opposition affords James the opportunity to celebrate his heroine, to awaken in the reader not just pity for Milly Theale, but a sense of her power. We begin to discover the terms of that opposition and its significance for James as we consider the author's remark in his notebook about the effect of that conflict upon Merton Densher: "In the light of how exquisite the dead girl was [Densher] sees how little exquisite is the living."[6]

In this sentence James sketches the resolution for his action and points us toward an understanding of a basic element of his design, one that has seldom received much attention from critics of the novel. Nor did James intend that we should dwell too long on an elementary fact which, although it underlies the opposition between the two women and subtly affects our response to that conflict, seems so at odds with the imputed sublimity with which both women pursue their respective passions. I refer to the fact that Milly and Kate, as devised by the author and apprehended by the reader, are in competition with one another. The competition is sexual and the vehicle for James's extended, if often oblique treatment of the conflicting powers which he identified with feminine sexuality. Milly is vulnerable and generous, and despite the similarities which I and many critics have noted between her and Isabel Archer, she more nearly resembles Nanda Brookenham and Fleda Vetch. But unlike Fleda and Nanda, Milly triumphs at the end of her story, the reason being that she is more, not less vulnerable and generous than the other two women. Her

6. *The Notebooks,* p. 173.

triumph has less to do with the probabilities of realistic fiction than with James's determination to celebrate what he saw as intensely beautiful in his heroine's very exposure.

Kate Croy, on the other hand, is aggressive and manipulative. She descends from Madame Merle and Mrs. Brookenham, and taken by herself she is probably the single most impressive woman, after Isabel Archer, whom the author created. And, as is the case with Milly, Kate Croy more perfectly represents the sexual tendency associated with her than any of her predecessors in James's fiction. She possesses the energy and the tactical skill of Madame Merle and Mrs. Brookenham: that capacity for initiating and sustaining action in the social order which we are encouraged to interpret as a function of their sexuality through observing the frequency with which that social skill is put to work to provide for, or protect a lover. But also, as we shall see, James makes more explicit in Kate Croy the connection between a social energy which is both splendid and coercive and the sexual source of that "talent for life."

The object of the competition between the two women is of course Merton Densher; it is he who will eventually choose between them and raise for James the memory of the dead girl over the presence of the living. Since Densher will choose between the two women, and since that choice both reflects the author's estimate of Milly and directs the reader toward a similar response, James was right to devote so much attention to Densher in the second half of the novel. His decision not to dramatize the last meeting between Milly and Densher, at which Milly is full of the sense that she has been tricked by another woman into imagining herself loved by that woman's lover is, I believe, part of James's overall strategy of avoiding a direct treatment of the sexual conflict between the two women. In the interview itself Milly makes no reference to her betrayal, as unwilling to appear tricked as she was to smell of the sickroom. James withholds from the reader this view of his young woman deceived until the force of the meeting has so worked on Densher's emotions that it induces him to choose Milly, or rather her memory, over Kate. Kate is the woman who is directly revealed in the novel as tricked, frustrated, deprived of her lover on any but the impossible terms of living with him in genteel poverty and memory of the departed dove. Before we give over to participation in this memory, in the moral and aesthetic apotheosis of Milly Theale, let us recall that she has clearly won the struggle that forms the basis for the novel's plot. She triumphs over Kate Croy, possesses Densher's love and loyalty, vindicates her sacrifice over the more conventional sacrifice with which Kate has earlier attempted to hold Densher. To assume that the victory is empty because she dies without enjoying Densher's love would be to engage in a very human, very practical kind of judgment which James would surely have found narrow. For in James's mind Milly Theale's best claim to Densher's love, the claim that is finally proved by her victory over Kate, is her willingness to give him up, even to facilitate the union of lover and rival. By such a stroke Milly Theale vindicates her own and her author's high estimate of her value, lives intensely in an individual, solitary act of choice, and devastates the moral and social landscape of those she leaves behind, those who, like Densher, Kate, and most of us, find it easier to survive in a community of partial guilt than in the splendid isolation of such shattering benevolence. But the story which concludes in this fashion is rooted in the struggle between the two women, a struggle which, throughout, is more a product of the Jamesian design than the probable acts of autonomous characters. It is to James's deployment of his two women in the design of their conflict that we must turn for an understanding of the evocative force of the novel's resolution.

I emphasize the degree of control exercised by James through his design of action and situation, because this is the only way of getting at the central paradox of the novel's effect upon us: whereas Densher's eventual choice of one woman over another is the chief device by which the author celebrates his heroine, the specific terms by which that choice is worked out suggest that Milly is superior precisely because she rises above sexual conflict and satisfaction. We applaud her heroism, her morality, or her sacrifice without being quite aware that the plot mechanism which elicits and shapes our approval is that of one woman's victory over another in a struggle for the man they both want. James here exploits the design of sexual conflict to command our respect for an individual act which he believed sufficiently intense and beautiful to transcend the order of sexual experience. In the light of how exquisite Milly has been we are intended to see how little exquisite are the passions and the desires of Kate Croy. Through the author's arrangement of the conflict between the two women, a conflict which Milly is simply unaware of until the end, we are to see the heroine's superiority to any of the tangible satisfactions which attract Kate Croy.

Kate Croy clearly does not anticipate the reversal that takes place in the last book of the novel. Throughout the long course of her conversations with Densher over Milly, it seems never to have occurred to her, except as a slightly comic possibility, that Densher could be won away from her by Milly. Indeed, most of the labor of her plot is the effort to make Densher simulate convincingly an admiration for the American girl. After she has made her remarkable pledge of affection to Densher in the second book of the novel, she never doubts that his commitment to her is at least as strong. After this scene, which of course comes before Milly herself has entered the novel, Kate reveals very little of her feelings toward Densher, a fact which considerably irritates the young man. What happens in James's presentation of Kate is that the excitement early established as a product of Kate's love for Densher is gradually transferred to the plan with which she intends to manipulate Milly and free herself from Aunt Maud's control. Densher becomes for her the most important instrument in her plan, this importance seeming to outweigh her original love for him as a man. And, lest this should be counted too severely against Kate in the reader's mind, there is considerable evidence to indicate that for James himself, Kate becomes most interesting when her fascination with the strategic uses of Densher begins to supplant her more conventional romantic interest in him.

What is made to occur in Kate's presentation in the novel is that her relatively conventional love for a man is made the stimulus for an ingenious and complex strategy for deception and manipulation. Literally, she undertakes to fool her aunt, Mrs. Stringham, and Milly herself in order that she might be free to marry Densher and rich enough to protect that marriage from financial or social insecurity. But the desire for Densher, the passion to fulfill herself sexually as a woman, is both expressed and, for James, enriched and made immeasurably more interesting as it evolves into a full-scale plan for deception, in which people and the occasions of social intercourse are used with great artistry. It is this which James, through Densher, calls Kate's "talent for life." The rendition of this talent in Kate Croy is James's most thorough treatment of those powers of imagination and will which seemed to him the most interesting manifestations of a mature, aggressive sexuality.

In the first two books of *The Wings of the Dove,* Kate is seen as threatened by several varieties of the commonplace. Her father laughs off her high pledge of filial piety and pushes her back toward Maud Lowder. Her sister Marian claims not only part of Kate's inheritance but a promissory note on the fortune Kate is to acquire when she satisfies her aunt by marrying Lord Mark. Moreover, Kate's meeting with her sister, like the interview with her father which begins the novel, suggests that unless Kate submits completely to her aunt she will plunge immediately into what James depicts as the dingy world of the ordinary and the undistinguished. We mark the author's distaste for such an environment in his description of Lionel Croy's tailoring and such passages as the following, in which lower middle class life is held up by the fingertips to be briefly examined.

> It was after the children's dinner, which was also their mother's, but which their aunt mostly contrived to keep from ever becoming her own luncheon; and the two young women were still in the presence of the crumpled table-cloth, the dispersed pinafores, the scraped dishes, the lingering odour of boiled food. Kate had asked with ceremony if she might put up a window a little, and Mrs. Condrip had replied without it that she might do as she liked. She often received such enquiries as if they reflected in a manner on the pure essence of her little ones. (I, 36)

Even Kate's love for Densher, which James never intended to be thought of as anything but real by the reader, is dealt with ironically. The two have met, we are told, at a party "given at a 'gallery' hired by a hostess who 'fished with big nets,' " nets which on this occasion have captured "a Spanish dancer, understood to be at that moment the delight of the town, an American reciter, the joy of a kindred people, an Hungarian fiddler, the wonder of the world at large." They meet by chance later on the subway, Densher approaching her seat by seat, until "at Notting Hill Gate Kate's right-hand neighbour descended, whereupon Densher popped straight into that seat." Densher himself is described in terms that suggest that although he is clearly a gentleman and "generally sound and generally pleasant," the essence of his character at this stage is that he resists any particular claim to attention. Later in the novel, we will grasp the importance of this fact, as Densher's amiable willingness to have the lines of his character sketched in make him an admirable measure for James of the value invested in both Milly Theale and Kate Croy. But for the moment he is simply an ordinary young man, "longish, leanish, fairish," who can always be expected to fit in.

What this means is that Kate's love for Densher, which the reader is encouraged to take as a prime motive for her later deception of Milly Theale, is openly regarded by the author as commonplace and slightly comic before opportunities for strategy begin to present themselves to Kate. Even the first pledge she makes to Densher, their engagement at the end of the second book of the novel, is delivered to quiet Densher's insistence that they marry at once, and to give Kate time to consider a plan for tricking Mrs. Lowder. We must distinguish between what actually animates the young woman in the course of action she undertakes, and the motive which James encourages us to accept because it corresponds to a traditional idea of what should motivate young women, and because our interest in Kate on these grounds can be exploited by James to sustain an interest in her on his terms. She is made to act as she does in the novel through James's desire to launch her out of the commonplace surroundings in which we first see her. She will, by herself, initiate an action calling for the greatest possible determination and subtlety. James considers the energy and the intelligence called forth from the character by the effort to deceive first Mrs. Lowder and then Milly Theale a sufficiently absorbing and intense object for the reader's attention. He does not so consider the progress of a love for Merton Densher, unenlivened by anything but the feelings which that love was liable to stimulate in either of the two. James lets the reader take this love as a primary motive in his dark heroine, but only on the condition that once granted our pretext, we will attend carefully to the energy and the skill with which Kate seeks to elevate her relations with Densher from a social and economic level which both she and James regard as banal and undistinguished.

Her difficulty, carefully orchestrated by James, is that, fixed in the design of polar contrast with Milly Theale, she is unable finally to escape the consequences of her own sexuality, however far she may advance in social or economic power. Let us recall that in his early notebook speculations about his story, James decisively rejected the development of a sexual relationship between his heroine and the young man who was to be kind to her. In James's mind such a development would have partially released Milly from her dilemma, that of wanting and being denied "life," and, correspondingly, allowed the reader some relief from his contemplation of the total frustration of ordinary human desires.

> I see [the young man] as having somehow to risk something, to lose something, to sacrific something in order to be kind to her, and to do it without a reward, for the poor girl, even if he loved her, has no life to give him in return: no life and no personal, no physical surrender, for it seems to me that one must represent her as too ill for *that* particular case. It has bothered me in thinking of the little picture—this idea of the physical possession, the brief physical, passional rapture which at first appeared essential to it; bothered me on account of the ugliness, the incongruity, the nastiness, *en somme,* of the man's 'having' a sick girl: also on account of something rather pitifully obvious and vulgar in the presentation of such a remedy for her despair—and such a remedy

only. 'Oh, she's dying without having had it? Give it to her and let her die'—that strikes me as sufficiently second-rate. Doesn't a greater prettiness, as well as a better chance for a story, abide in her being already too ill for that, and in his being able merely to show her some delicacy of kindness, let her think that they might have loved each other *ad infinitum* if it hadn't been too late.[7]

As it would have been, for James, second-rate to allow Milly's dilemma to be broken by actual if temporary sexual happiness with Densher, so also would it be, as we have seen, second-rate for Kate Croy to content herself with marriage to a poor journalist. Kate's force and her interest as a character in her own right stem from her decision to evade Densher's "Marry me now, as I am," in an effort to have everything, wealth, social power, and the freedom rather than the grim constraint of sexuality represented by her sister. But since Milly's value as a woman is conceived of as essentially transcending the sexual, as indeed confounding the "second-rate" associations attached to such fulfillment, Kate Croy must be represented as finally reduced to the sexual, her value as a woman defined by her attempt to hold Densher's loyalty by going to bed with him.

As we have seen in the notebook entry which I have quoted above, James considered and then rejected a sexual "remedy for [Milly's] despair." It is impossible not to be struck by the distaste with which the author contemplates sexual union between Densher and the "sick girl," and difficult to avoid speculation about obsessive elements in James's own personality.[8] What I should rather stress are the consequences within the novel of James's emphatic rejection of this partial remedy for his heroine. Not only is the possibility for sexual satisfaction to be disposed of in the past—Milly is "already too ill for that"—but also the resolution of her relations with Densher is here dimly foreshadowed as an action which at once radically opposes the sexual, and preempts a good deal of its evocative power over the reader. Milly, exposed to death and therefore too ill for sexual passion, turns toward that death when she learns of her betrayal. She does so, however, with a gesture of benevolence toward Densher which binds him more absolutely to her memory than he could ever have been bound, by sexual passion, to the living Milly Theale. Milly's "sacrifice" is the product of a solitary act of consciousness and will, and figures for James as the realization of values implicit in her from his first conception of her character.

7. *Ibid.*, pp. 169-70.
8. Geismar, *Henry James*, p. 222.

James has here attempted to enlist for his heroine something of the intensity of sexual surrender while imputing to her sacrifice a value which transcends and negates the sexual. Kate Croy, whose identity is essentially established in the novel's polar design, is therefore made to undergo a descent from the imaginative energy which animates her scheme to the source of that power, her sexuality. And as Milly's value is certified by the transformation effected in Densher, so also does James purposely allow Kate to be demeaned by the young man's dull insistence that she give him a reason for continuing the plot.

James does not entirely succeed in his celebration of Milly's sacrifice at the expense of Kate's. The difficulty is that the reader, having taken note of Kate's vitality and perceived her sexual attractiveness as inseparable from her powers of will and imagination, finds it less easy than does James to relinquish her in favor of a transcendental passion. We deal here not with the moral terms established within the fiction—for according to these Kate is amply guilty—but rather with the claims made upon our sympathy by Kate's passion for life. That passion is formidably rendered in Kate Croy, so successfully in fact that it does not entirely submit to the function for which James has placed it within the design of his novel: that of representing as "second-rate" the ideals of social and sexual power standing in contrast to, and transcended by Milly Theale's sacrifice.

Kate's accession to Densher's demand, her only alternative to giving up his support for her strategy, actually signals the end of her effective control of Densher. And from this episode to the end of the novel the point of view is Densher's, his consciousness the context in which James prepares for Milly's eventual triumph. What is important to note about the change that occurs in Densher, however, is that it is inadequately described by the term "moral," at least as we use that term to signify a standard for human conduct. What happens to Densher is much closer to the phenomenon described by the term "transformation," or, in the religious context supplied in this final section in the form of powerful supportive metaphor, "conversion."[9] Milly's act of generosity, focused and intensified for James and Densher by contrast with Kate's sexual "sacrifice," effects a qualitative change in Densher's life, in his very manner of perceiving reality. It transforms him from a young man of direct, basically simple emotions, adaptable to the uses and the ways of society, to a subdued and yet

9. For an analysis of Densher's transformation in terms of the psychological and moral qualities attributed to the young man, see Krook, *The Ordeal of Consciousness,* pp. 221-31.

still fervent celebrant of the ideal figured in Milly's transcendence over desire. This desire is now and has been throughout the novel both financial and sexual. Milly overcomes her humiliation to the extent that she can give the two lovers the money they desired. She overcomes what is for James, and ultimately for Densher, the relative banality of sexual satisfaction by giving herself to Densher in this way and in this way alone.

What remains is to note the manner in which James orchestrates the interplay of thought and feeling in Densher's consciousness so as to represent the qualitative change that occurs in the man, and to celebrate Milly not only as beautiful in herself, but also as the source of power sufficiently strong to effect such radical change in Densher. The process by which he arrives at virtual reverence for the memory of Milly Theale is intended to induce a similar response in the reader.

The essence of Densher's development here is that it is not progressive and incremental, the normal characteristics of moral change, even that of a very radical type. After he has slept with Kate, Densher re-affirms his intention to continue acting his part in her strategy, very significantly observing to himself, however, that Kate's sacrifice to him, which was supposed to bolster his sense of masculine control, seems actually to have bound him closer to Kate's will. He nevertheless proceeds to rationalize, yet again, his own part in the deception of Milly, and in such rationalization he remains relatively secure until he catches sight of Lord Mark, who has of course returned to Venice to tell Milly the truth. The sight of Lord Mark, joined with silence from the palace, throws Densher into a panic of guilt and bitter recrimination against the villainous Lord Mark, the bearer of the truth. "You couldn't drop on the poor girl," Densher thinks to himself, "without . . . being brutal." (II, 265)

Despite the fact that James's irony in this section of the novel prevents the reader from being taken in by Densher's several strategies of self-justification, it is interesting to note the way in which James has used the character of Lord Mark, made suitably sinister and associated in Milly's mind with the figure of the crass fortune hunter, to protect Merton Densher from some of the distaste with which the reader might otherwise regard him. Densher is not only a character in the novel; he is the essential context for the glorification of Milly Theale, and so James's rhetoric operates to save him from the dislike we are eventually encouraged to feel toward Kate Croy, and which an objective estimate of Densher's actual part in the deception might gain for him as well. We have before encountered the use of minor characters, such as Henrietta Stackpole and Susan Stringham, positioned in the story so as to distract what otherwise might be the reader's sense of the comic or the absurd in the actions of the heroine. Here Lord Mark is used to ensure that Densher preserves the degree of purity necessary for his eventual conversion and use as a celebrant by the author.

Densher later further eases his sense of guilt in his conversation with Mrs. Stringham, that lady by now uneasy enough over her part in Milly's deception to be eager to join Densher in condemnation of Lord Mark. (II, 283-286) When Sir Luke arrives from London to treat Milly for the last time, Densher seems finally to grasp the enormity of the fact that Milly is going to die, that she has lived out the European experience in this knowledge. The dominant tone of his reflections at this point is less panicky or recriminatory, although he still insists that a major part of his difficulty was that "there had been, in all the case, too many women." Instead he is stunned and saddened by the final realization of Milly's imminent death, a realization which Densher finds it so hard to bear that he is grateful to Sir Luke, who lets him off by not enquiring for particulars about the shock which Milly has experienced. (II, 294-309)

Now these emotions which I have described, panic, guilt, the desire for relief through accusations against Lord Mark and the protection of Sir Luke, and sorrow at the prospect of Milly's death—these are what characterize Densher at the end of Book Nine. They are thoroughly consistent with the lines of his character drawn in the earlier section of the novel, and they seem to me to be quite justly characterized as the emotional accompaniments of a particular kind of moral discovery, the abrupt recognition on the part of a man who has lazily prolonged his own innocence that he is indeed capable of evil.

Now the Densher who appears in Book Ten, that is, Densher after his final interview with Milly, has not simply progressed a few stages further in his moral education. He has, rather, been struck by a sense that his actions are less significant for their moral consequences than as occasions for the reception of some spiritual benefit, some peculiar form of secular grace which has come to him, like the old Calvinist's saving grace of election, quite apart from the moral value of his own acts.

> He saw a young man far off and in a relation inconceivable, saw him hushed, passive, staying his breath, but half understanding, yet dimly concious of something immense and holding himself painfully together

not to lose it. The young man at these moments so seen was too distant and too strange for the right identity; and yet, outside, afterwards, it was his own face Densher had known. He had known then at the same time what the young man had been conscious of, and he was to measure after that, day by day, how little he had lost. At present there with Mrs. Lowder he knew he had gathered all—that passed between them mutely as in the intervals of their associated gaze they exchanged looks of intelligence.This was as far as association could go, but it was far enough when she knew the essence. The essence was that something had happened to him too beautiful and too sacred to describe. He had been, to his recovered sense, forgiven, dedicated, blessed; but this he couldn't coherently express. (II, 342-43)

The scene which Densher remembers in this passage is that of his last visit with Milly. The effects of that visit are visible in the scene which opens Book Ten, indeed in the words of Kate with which the scene and the chapter open: "Then it has been—what do you say? a whole fortnight?—[since Densher's return to London] without your making a sign?" (II, 313) For the first time in the novel Densher here affects a sense and a manner of superiority toward Kate, that superiority deriving from his last visit with Milly. Moreover, Densher, who has earlier submitted himself to instruction in the arts of society administered by Kate, here reverses the roles, becomes himself her instructor in the meaning of such qualities as Milly possessed.

> "Did she show anything of her feeling? I mean," Kate explained, "of her feeling of having been misled . . ."
> "She showed nothing but her beauty and her strength."
> "Then," his companion asked, "what's the use of her strength?"
> He seemed to look about for a use he could name; but he had soon given it up. "She must die, my dear, in her own extraordinary way."
> (II, 329)

There are many such instances in these last two interviews between Densher and Kate of James making use of Densher's radical change to express, in opposition to Kate's "talent for life," the ideals of "beauty" and "strength" as themselves inherently noble, even more so for their resistance to "use." And however splendid Kate's "talent for life" may have been, it is made to suffer by comparison in Densher's mind with the beauty and the strength conveyed by Milly's dying "in her extraordinary way."

But the major evidence of the radical transformation which has occurred in Densher, and the rhetorical use which James makes of that change to celebrate Milly Theale, is provided for us in the novel's last scene. For here Densher has devised an action which is essentially a ritualistic enactment, insofar as he is able to duplicate it, of the sacrifice with which Milly died. Not only does he himself wish to renounce the fortune left him by Milly; he wishes Kate to join with him in this refusal. To do so would signify for James and for Densher a kind of purification, but more than this; it would provide what Densher calls a "test" for Kate Croy, a test whereby that woman of talent and desire might make a symbolic deference to the woman who transcended both. Densher's suggestion that they return the money along with "an absolutely kind letter" is, after all, only a suggestion, one that Kate need not accept. She may take Densher without the money or the money without Densher, but she may not have both. But by his leaving it up to her Densher recreates symbolically that subtle combination of helplessness and power, the polarity which has throughout defined the character of Milly Theale. And finally, his act has about it all of the isolated sublimity which we have learned to associate with the figure and the sacrifice of Milly Theale. It is Densher's gesture, not of moral retribution, but rather of symbolic tribute to the memory of a dead woman, with whose *memory*, as the living woman realizes, Densher is in love.

7

THE LIMITS OF DESIGN

Henry James was deeply moved by a certain type of experience, the characteristic design of which appears in all of his major work. Its persistence, in forty years of work by an intensely professional writer, suggests his belief that the reader could be similarly moved by the design of radical conflict. A recurrent pattern in the arrangement of a novelist's material may of course reveal much about his attitude toward that material, or the audience toward which it is directed. And it is possible to deduce from a study of form a writer's general assumptions concerning the interplay of social and moral forces in the society in which he lives.

Our difficulty with James has been that we have been too quick to make such deductions, and too dependent upon them. We have not yet thoroughly dealt with James's form, the arrangement of parts in his fiction, as a reflection of his simple but shrewdly implemented desire to move, surprise, engage his reader. Regarding James as a major commentator upon the manners and morals of his day, we have sought in his work consistency and clarity of a kind essential to moral or psychological analysis, but not necessarily and not always requisite for the telling of his tale. Moreover, there are at present signs that as our own social and moral attitudes move further away from the loose collection of cultural views deducible from James's fiction (and honored by critics of the 1950s) we may be forced to re-encounter Henry James in the role of social arbiter, the exponent of values we now feel the need to condemn. Whereas James was extravagantly praised during the fifties for his moral profundity, he now begins to acquire an opposite, if equally weighty celebrity as a subverter of the collective life, an imperialist for the American self.[1]

What I have attempted to demonstrate in the preceding chapters is that a reasonably strict attention to James's strategy as a storyteller may be of more use to us in determining what James intended and achieved in his fiction than debate over social or moral paradigms which, although they may be constructed from James's material, tell us little about the actual manner in which the author worked over and developed that material.

Even on those occasions when such elements of his tale as action, situation or character seem clearly ordered to impress upon the reader a larger view of society, it will be seen that this view is ultimately designed to justify and defend the Jamesian artist engaged in his characteristic lonely, intense observation. This is the case in *The Princess Casamassima* and *The Tragic Muse,* novels which are in the end remarkable not for their social breadth but rather for the manner in which the illusion of a social mechanism is created to threaten and thereby sanction and exalt the efforts of the isolated imagination, pretty clearly that of Henry James in thin disguise. James's generalized views on society and moral and psychological growth originate in the seriousness with which he took himself as a particular kind of writer, and not in attempts either to represent or to prescribe a real social organism.

The primary source then for James's view of society was not so much his observation of English and American life as his strong intuitive sense of the needs of that "consciousness" which he exploited in his craft and simultaneously celebrated in his fiction. "Society" arises as mingled possibility and threat—almost entirely threat in the latter stages of his career—in which and against which the Jamesian consciousness struggles. For all of the realistic conventions of James's art, this "society" exists not as a representation of observable, objective conditions, but first and foremost, as the fictive medium created precisely to serve the needs of Hyacinth, Isabel, Maisie, and the rest. And

1. Anderson, *The Imperial Self.*

as conceived of by James, especially in the Notebooks, what these characters primarily demand is that the reader sympathize, wonder, be impressed by the extraordinary quality of their lives. This explains why social and psychological facts in the work of Henry James can strike us, at first, as rich and plausible, and then, upon reflection, as contrived, in some crucial way foreign to ordinary experience. These facts are contrived, subtly and often almost imperceptibly. Contrivance is the nature of art, but the key fact here is that James contrives for the purpose of shaping and developing the reactions of his reader, and only instrumentally to create a plausibly detailed version of reality. Thus, James may succeed in moving us powerfully by means of the story of Isabel Archer, an action which upon subsequent reflection seems too neatly contrived for accurate representation. The answer is that the action exists not for that purpose, but rather as a fictive structure designed to display, embellish, take care of Isabel Archer as she encounters the reader. In this the contrivance has succeeded. When we later object that a given sequence or arrangement of details seems improbable, because, for example, it lacks any suggestion of the sheer randomness of life, we have merely succeeded in extracting ourselves from an imaginative world in which every element is connected to every other by an intricate system of internal reference, the rationale for which is its affective rather than its representational force.

And there is a world described here, described in considerable and usually satisfying detail. Most immediately it is comprised of objects, gestures, movements, the reaction of characters to one another, states of mind and feelings in the people presented. These are solid, specific notations of social and psychological experience. This kind of effect is the product of James's own early dissatisfaction with, on the one hand, the bare allegories of Hawthorne, and on the other, the flat comic characterization in the work of Dickens. Underlying the aesthetic decisions which James made as a young writer was his conviction that the role of the artist was that of minute and scrupulous observation, and the sense that such a role was as active, perhaps more intensely so, than ordinary involvement in "life." Hence, the thoroughly furnished world of the James novel, the rich and absorbing system of social and moral detail which strikes the reader so forcefully as, for example, Isabel walks onto the lawn at Gardencourt. But again, these details, varied as they are, exist to serve James's conception of what is extraordinary and intense in the lives of his major characters. And the aesthetic consequence of James's persistent desire that his tales embody the extraordinary is that the elements of these tales, including the realistic facts we have been discussing, must be subjected to a degree of control which they would not have were they items of representational art. Details, like the action of which they are a part, subserve the essential demand of intensity, the result of James's personal need to display the act of imagination, or consciousness, as more vital than any other form of conduct.

A study of James's reaction to the outbreak of the First World War, or his bewildered response to American immigration in the first decade of the twentieth century, strongly suggests that James had no more than a casual and conventional understanding of forces underlying both American and European society. In this connection it appears that Yvor Winters was correct when he claimed that James's comprehension of the specifics of American social life was less extensive than Edith Wharton's.[2]

Nor did England, with what James regarded as its superior social density, actually provide him with additional material, that is, material to be taken on its own terms. Rather he found there a freedom precisely similar to that which he granted to his own heroes and heroines: a freedom based on the dual assurance that one is surrounded by the artifacts of history and culture, while yet—and here we come again to the animating illusion, the chief convention, of James's work— untouched and unimpeded in the center of one's existence, by the nagging, irreducible, or simply opaque facts of place, history, or culture. With such assurance James had the context for his tales, the whole scheme of controllable reference to particulars of social and moral life whose function it was to be charged by the tension he could generate with the radical polarities of his action.

James's fascination with the design of polar conflict and his successful employment of it in his fiction suggest that he ought to be regarded as a very skilled practitioner in a distinctive genre of his own, a fusion of American allegorical romance and European realism. Jamesian "allegory" is not supposed to instruct, but rather to elicit from the reader an intense, and at times, almost religious appreciation for states of mind and types of experience which stirred such a response in James himself. James made full use of the affective power of allegorical form, while substituting deep, subjective convictions of his own for the traditional dogma of allegory, convictions which, I have argued, arose out of his sense of the possibilities and limits of his own particular kind of art. His novels constitute an implicit appeal for,

2. Winters, *In Defense of Reason*, p. 309.

and justification of consciousness, individualism, and freedom, as against social or collective action and sexual passion.

Consciousness and the desire for freedom are not primarily the instruments of social and moral experience for James's major figures. Rather they are values in and by themselves, and it was to intensify and thereby celebrate these values that James fashioned his characteristic design of polar conflict. Such conflict offers the Jamesian hero an escape from the degree of compromise and adaptation usually required of the protagonist in realistic fiction. Compromise and adaptation were unsatisfactory to James, not as available options in life, but rather as strategies for fiction. Once again, the operative principle for James is aesthetic, not social or moral. Compromise lessens intensity, reduces the effect of the extraordinary in character or situation. Common in life, it tends toward diffusion or waste in art, and is thus to be employed only to sustain that minimal illusion of reality without which, James calculated, he could not hope to secure an immediate hold upon the reader.

For the hero, so severe is the threat to his freedom or consciousness that these ideals are made to seem wholly admirable as ends in themselves. They are not prerequisites for an action ultimately to be judged in accordance with social or moral standards. James represents and celebrates a type of radical individualism in which the passion for knowledge and freedom is idealized through polar conflict with personal and social forces conceived of by James as innately antagonistic: greed, aggression, sexual passion, collective action. The result in his major work was that the heroic took the form of a solitary and intense act of will or consciousness opposed by, and therefore isolated from the social, material, and sexual ambitions with which the realistic novel traditionally concerns itself.

Much is to be gained by increased attention to rhetorical aspects of James's art. By rhetoric I mean the whole series of fictive strategies James employed in an effort to evoke and control the interest and the sympathy of the reader. I have dealt with relatively obvious strategies, but an extension of the type of stylistic analysis made by Richard Poirer in *The Comic Sense of Henry James* would yield us much more precise knowledge of the manner in which James achieved some of his most subtle and intricate effects in the response of the reader. To make such a study feasible two things would have to occur, the second considerably more difficult than the first. The first, is that we would have to relax our hold upon the conviction that James was a writer relatively indifferent to the specific emotional reactions of his audience. The second problem is a more difficult one. To make a really fruitful study of the rhetoric of Henry James, or of any comparably difficult writer, we need some sort of basic study of the psychology of the reader's response to fiction. Norman Holland's recent *The Dynamics of Literary Response* indicates a growing interest in the problem.

We ought to relax our claims for James as a consistently profound psychologist and moralist. As I have tried to demonstrate, it is possible to discover in James's most important novels a concern prior to the moral, social, or psychological interests in terms of which the novels are usually discussed. Too often James's work has provided a context for moral and psychological theorizing which may be interesting but which in fact tells us little about either his major interests or his achievements as a writer. If admitting that some of the most "profound" ideas attributed to James are in fact literary constructs designed to engage the reader's attention and emotions means cutting back on his current reputation, then we ought to do so.

James made use of realistic technique to enrich—while the design of his action intensified—the experience represented for us in the stories of Isabel Archer, Milly Theale, and his other "free spirits." His design of polar conflict was, as we have seen, an extremely effective means of eliciting and sustaining for his characters the sympathy of the reader. But at the same time, it was precisely this design, similar to the form of allegory, which, when joined with minutely observed realistic detail, could seriously flaw James's art.

To understand why this is so we need once again to emphasize the peculiar instability of the synthesis which is the Jamesian novel, a point perhaps easier to grasp if we restrict our attention for the moment to a typical scene. On the one hand, the surface elements of the scene, whether they be Isabel's physical movement through the gallery at Gardencourt, or Strether's reflections on one aspect of Chad's transformation, appeal for their validity to our ordinary assumptions about reality: for example, that it is concrete, multiform, contingent, temporal. Thus, our interest and attention are solicited by means of the standard conventions of realistic fiction, and we are thereby invited to a sympathetic proximity with the characters impossible and undesirable for a work of art governed by assumptions further removed from those we normally employ in our own lives. Moreover, it would appear that the principal effect of the use of such conventions in a James novel, unlike, say, the effect of George Eliot's observance of them, is not so much mimetic fidelity as the pleasurable sense of having observed much and well. Which is merely to say that with his realistic detail James's chief success is to produce in his reader an approximation of the author's own original delight, so abundantly revealed in the Notebooks.

But if James's intention in his novels is not merely to imitate, neither is it simply to provide his reader with the pleasure of rich and discriminating observation. Isabel and Strether are meant to be extraordinary, an effect chiefly measurable by the intensity generated in their presentation, and the excitement awakened in the reader. Now the effect of the extraordinary in the James novel is achieved primarily through his management of plot, not just by according to his characters a remarkable freedom and self-consciousness in the business of choice, but also by arranging the antecedents, the terms, and the consequences of that choice in very strict and controlled fashion. The chief sign of this latter strategy is the design of polarity examined in the preceding chapters.

Given the sympathetic attention of the reader, itself nourished by the pleasures of observation, the radical polarities of the Jamesian action could indeed produce the desired intensity of effect, greater perhaps than that achieved by any novelist of James's time. But the danger which James faced was that the synthesis would come apart, that the elements of realistic and what I have called allegorical art would cease to supplement one another and begin to arouse contradictory and irreconcilable expectations on the part of the reader. The Jamesian synthesis was peculiarly unstable because the satisfaction afforded the reader by realistic detail could produce a demand for, paradoxically, a *less* conclusive, or ingeniously reversed, or schematic resolution than that produced by such allegorical strategies as the polar design of action. Under such pressure the contrivance begins to dissolve, typically leaving the reader with the bewildered sense of the falsely portentous, the implausible, or perhaps an obsessive hero inexplicably endorsed by his creator.

This occasional failure to control expectations aroused in the reader by his combination of realistic and allegorical techniques accounts, I believe, for the major flaws in James's fiction. Although only once, in *The Sacred Fount,* was the failure so serious as to destroy the novel, there are signs of the problem in most of the works we have here considered. In *The Spoils of Poynton,* for example, James became so fascinated with the evocative power of his design that, in pursuit of its logic, he frustrates the reader's expectations and his sense of probability, both founded on the earlier, detailed and realistic treatment of Fleda Vetch and Owen Gereth. In *The Princess Casamassima,* James discovers the manner in which his polar design may be used for essentially polemical purposes, for pleading rather than rendering the case for the fine consciousness in opposition to the claims of a collective experience. In the end, all of Hyacinth's story is absorbed into the argument, the exigencies of which demand that Hyacinth suffer prolonged victimization, and in the process sacrifice his claim upon the reader's interest and sympathy. The working out of the Jamesian design in *The Awkward Age* does not so severely flaw the work, but it does produce a novel quite different from that which most critics have taken it to be. Ultimately James's chief interest lies in neither social nor moral issues but rather with the excitement to be generated by a conflict between antagonistic forms of sexuality. The novel's intention is to stimulate and balance in the reader an interest in these forms, represented by Mrs. Brook and Nanda, and in this the novel seems to me to succeed. Admitting this, however, we must also admit that the schematic treatment of sex in the novel signifies no real attempt to relate this experience to larger social or moral concerns, but rather a very shrewd exploitation of the inherent interest it has for us—and for James.

There remain Isabel Archer and Milly Theale and the control exercised over their histories by James's polar design. *The Portrait of a Lady* represents James's most successful employment of his design, whereas *The Wings of the Dove,* if carefully enough considered, forces the reader to confront the implications of Jamesian rhetoric as both a strategy in his fiction and as an expression of his fundamental attitudes toward experience.

Isabel's case is the easier. The design by which she moves between the polarities of radical freedom and submission accommodates a very substantial amount of realistic detail, thereby shaping our interest in Isabel as a particular young woman, while ensuring that we retain the sense that her story is "extraordinary," that is, not finally reducible to the concrete facts of her experience. Particularly in the early sections of the novel, Isabel is developed with a solidity and a gaiety of specification which fix our interest in her. But, at the same time, the novel's structure determines that our eventual response to Isabel's marriage will be pity and surprise at the radical change in her fortunes and only secondarily a sense of Isabel's personal responsibility for that change.

The working out of James's design in *The Wings of the Dove* solicits from the reader a response he may find more difficult to make.

On the one hand, the polar design figured in James's initial conception of Milly, that of a young woman on the threshold of life but condemned to death, is worked out in the novel with great power and beauty. But, as we have seen, the final intensification of this design is achieved through conflict between Milly and Kate Croy, both women clearly devised to represent qualitatively different types of experience. Milly's vindication and her triumph in the end signal for James and for Densher the superiority of an experience marked by intense, isolated, and transcending passion. The reader, however, cannot help but perceive the manner in which this passion levels as it transcends the ordinary landscape of desire and guilt. The ascent of the dove would appear to effect much more than a moral revelation to the pair who have victimized her. Milly's celebration in the novel necessitates a systematic reduction of the type of experience figured in the person of Kate Croy, an experience which is contingent and problematic, shaped by continuities of social and sexual life. The Jamesian design solicits the reader's approval for the sudden, shattering dismissal of all of this, but the very success with which James has rendered Kate Croy makes such a response impossible.

APPENDIX

James's Design and the Critics

Although they have differed widely in particulars of interpretion, most critics of Henry James have assented to the following general propositions about his art. That art was fundamentally imitative, its object being the internal life of his characters. He traced the process by which ideas, emotions, and desires interact under the stress of a given moral or social problem. The Jamesian techniques of fiction are to be seen as instruments of representation which become more and more refined as the author deals with the increasingly complex internal histories of his characters. The most important of the techniques are strict control of point of view, alternation between scene and summary description, and the supportive use of imagery. James, it is conventionally said, brings to its richest point of development in fiction the genre of psychological portraiture, and he does it by dramatizing the elements of his picture. We observe directly the interplay of thought and feeling and are consequently freed from our reliance upon the normative commentary of the traditional narrator.

I have summarized what I take to be the major assumptions underlying the criticism of James's fiction, and since in my argument I try to demonstrate that these assumptions are not a wholly sufficient guide to the understanding of James's work, I should indicate my posi-

141

tion with reference to critics who support, and those who at least partially dissent from, the ideas I have summarized. I shall briefly mention some of the most respected of James's critics, men in great part responsible for our appreciation of James as a major writer. As the body of my essay shows, I take issue with them only when I think it demonstrable that their view of James as psychologist and moralist obscures another equally important aspect of the man's art: his fascination with the evocative power of the design of polar conflict. Further, my list of critics is highly selective, my intention here being to test my thesis against a group of critics who represent broad and major tendencies of Jamesian criticism and scholarship.

F. O. Matthiessen's study, *Henry James: The Major Phase,* places James within the Emersonian tradition. He is occasionally skeptical about James's achievements as a psychologist and moral analyst, his chief objection being to the author's management of Adam Verver in *The Golden Bowl,* a novel which "forces upon our attention too many flagrant lapses in the way things happen both in the personal and in the wider social sphere."[1] But elsewhere, Matthiessen, attempting to revive James's reputation after Parrington's attack, lays too much stress upon the Jamesian types of behavior and moral values which he finds, "oddly enough, not at all remote" from that new synthesis of "political economy and theology" sought by Matthiessen's own generation of critics.[2] Matthiessen bends his knowledge of American cultural history and psychological and aesthetic theory to an investigation of James's "profound sense of moral values."[3] In my view, Matthiessen is both the most stimulating of James's critics and the source of the modern tendency to exaggerate James's practice of psychological and moral analysis. Matthiessen has little to say about the implication of James's fascination with evocative action or about his attempts to orchestrate the responses of his readers.

Although my own study does not focus on biographical detail, I have profited greatly from Leon Edel's biography of James. For me, the chief value of the work has been its ample demonstration of the degree to which James's typical themes arise out óf the tensions and uncertainties of his own experience. To cite only one example, from *The Conquest of London,* Edel's discussion of the need felt by both William and Henry to liberate themselves from the benign control of their parents helps us to understand Henry's persistent belief in the

1. Matthiessen, *James,* p. 104.
2. *Ibid.,* p. 151.
3. *Ibid.,* xi.

beauty and intensity of an act of free will, however disastrous the consequences of that act might be.[4] With Edel's research it is possible to free oneself from the notion that James was either perfectly detached or perfectly consistent in his treatment of ethical ideas in his fiction. On the other hand, Edel occasionally seems prepared to suggest that the chief interest of a Jamesian character derives from the clarity with which he or she displays some putative feature of James's own emotional history.

Christof Wegelin, in his book *The Image of Europe in Henry James,* deals with James's contrast between American and European attitudes, and remarks the fairy-tale-like quality of the plots which bring the two into conflict. But, whereas for Wegelin, the relevance of such conflict is finally that it was a "medium for projecting what [James] saw as psychological and moral realities,"[5] I would wish to examine more thoroughly the strategy of conflict itself, and the author's fascination with it.

Henry James: A Reader's Guide, by S. Gorley Putt, generally follows the lead of F. R. Leavis in his primary emphasis on James's skill as moralist and social commentator. Putt is much less solemn in his appraisal of James than many American critics, values the humor and broad tolerance conveyed by the author's style, and distrusts mythic and religious interpretations of James's later work. He cites numerous examples of James's fondness for balanced opposition in his work, regarding this as a reflection of the author's own "geminian personality." Neither this characteristic of James's art, nor his apparently obsessive interest in what Putt calls the theme of "marriage as an avoidable disaster," can tempt Putt from a conventional reading of the novels as psychological and social realism.

I have profited from the spirit, if not always the letter, of Quentin Anderson's *The American Henry James.* Like most who have read this book, I cannot accept many of Anderson's emblematic readings of events and characters in the novels: I cannot see Lionel Croy as the Devil;[6] still less can I hold Susan Stringham in my mind in the role of the "rational or the scientific mind."[7] More seriously, to read the novels as Anderson reads them, as vehicles for the elder Henry James's theological system, is to submerge under a heavy weight the author and the spirit so admirably discussed by Poirier, the James whose wit

4. Edel, *James: The Conquest,* pp. 135-156.
5. Wegelin, *The Image of Europe,* p. 88.
6. Anderson, *The American,* p. 241.
7. *Ibid.,* p. 269.

and grace of spirit affect us so engagingly. But I value Anderson's book for its emphasis on elements in James which, it seems to me, are not adequately accounted for in the standard psychological and moral analysis. I refer specifically to James's essentially celebratory treatment of a quasi-mystical consciousness in his major characters, his reluctance, except in *The Bostonians,* to center the experience of his characters in social institutions or the historical process, and finally, his very stylized, even allegorical plots.

Two recent works of structural analysis have sharpened our sense of the skill with which James arranged his material within his novels. Walter Isle, in his *Experiments in Form: Henry James's Novels, 1896-1901,* investigates a subject often alluded to by critics of James, but never thoroughly dealt with: the degree to which James experimented in the fiction of the late nineties with dramatic techniques learned while writing for the stage. Isle discusses the manner in which techniques like the structural division of material into acts, the alternation of scene and reflection, and the use of different types of dialogue were incorporated into such novels as *The Spoils of Poynton* and *What Maisie Knew.* He is principally interested in the forms of the novels as they subserve the demands of characterization. For example, he argues that the form of *The Spoils of Poynton* reflects the artistic and moral issues focused by the character of Fleda Vetch. Thus, the novel consists of four parts including an epilogue. The technique shifts from that of introspective narration in the first section through a later scenic dramatization appropriate to the heroine's increasingly confi- dent expression of her imagination. The novel concludes in the explosion of forces over which the fine consciousness of Fleda Vetch has no control. Isle's thesis is that James's experience as a dramatist equipped him with techniques and structural skill adequate to the task of representing the struggle of such morally sensitive characters as Fleda, Nanda Brookenham, and Maisie Farange, first to understand, then to preserve themselves within a hostile environment.

J. A. Ward's analysis of Jamesian structure, *The Search for Form,* is broader in scope than Isle's study and less concerned with the manner in which James's methods were shaped by specific experiences as a writer. Instead, Ward devotes the first section of his book to a summary description of a Jamesian theory of form, never articulated in its entirety by the author, but observable as a set of basic assumptions in his criticism of other novelists and in commentary on his own work. James's theory of form, according to Ward, may be described as a fusion of Classical (formalist) and Romantic (organic) elements. On the one hand, James delighted in the symmetrical arrangement of his material, a stylized and strictly controlled deployment of character, scene, and detail in an effort to achieve formal perfection and autonomy for his fiction. But on the other hand, Ward observes, James's fiction and criticism exhibit such elements of organic theory as a belief in the potentially limitless development of human personality and relations, and the calculated use of stylistic ambiguity reflecting a concern with problems of perception and knowledge. Having established this thematic frame for his analysis, Ward's technique is to examine such works as "Madame de Mauves," *The Europeans, The Princess Casamassima,* and *The Wings of the Dove* in an effort to determine whether James's stylized formal arrangement enhances the portrayal of his chosen subject. For Ward, following J. W. Beach, argues that the fundamental art of Henry James is that of portraiture, and he consequently regards action as a device for displaying the subject rather than for effecting substantial change in the characters. The subject of "Madame de Mauves" Ward takes to be moral rigidity, that of *The Europeans* is the clash between responsibility and opportunism, and, more doubtfully, the subject of *The Princess Casamassima* is London itself.

My study deals with several of the novels examined by Isle and Ward, and I share their assumption that an examination of James's structural techniques is one of the most fruitful approaches to his work. I differ from Isle in my belief that Jamesian form is less significant as a device for augmenting characterization than as a means of controlling the interest and sympathy of the reader. My objection to Ward's book, which I nonetheless think to be one of the best on the subject, is that in the end it exaggerates the importance of the classical element of James's artistic temperament. It thereby misses what is perhaps the most interesting paradox of James's art: that the author's very preoccupation with balanced and symmetrical elements of form may be seen not as the consequences of his commitment to faithful portraiture, but rather as the expression of his delight in the inherently evocative powers of extreme contrast. Ward, like many other recent critics of the author, slights the James of the Notebooks, in favor of the James of the Prefaces.

From Yvor Winters' essay on James in *In Defense of Reason,* I have adapted for my own use two ideas concerning the nature of James's art. The first is "that James is much more than a mere portrayer of the American abroad; his work partakes in a considerable measure of the allegorical character of Hawthorne."[8] It seemed to me that this suggestion could be most usefully followed by investigating the characteristic Jamesian action to determine whether its peculiar strength lay in its capacity for portraiture or for the rhetorical and celebratory functions typical of allegory.

Winters further describes James as a writer who attempted to depict the American moral sense in something like its pure form, that is, "divorced from any body of American manners."[9] My study argues that the specific values which James sought to depict and celebrate were freedom and consciousness, both of which he conceived of as most admirable in their pure form, that is, protected from the conventional social compulsion to finally resolve freedom and consciousness into choice and act. What I have called the Jamesian design evolved to depict and celebrate these pure values.

8. Winters, *In Defense of Reason*, p. 316.
9. *Ibid.*

BIBLIOGRAPHY

Allot, Miriam. "The Bronzino Portrait in *The Wings of the Dove.*" *Modern Language Notes,* LXVIII (Jan. 1953), 23-25.
_____. "Symbol and Image in the Later Work of Henry James." *Essays in Criticism,* III (July 1953), 321-336.
Anderson, Quentin. *The American Henry James.* New Brunswick, New Jersey: Rutgers University Press, 1957.
_____. *The Imperial Self: An Essay in American Literary and Cultural History.* New York: Alfred A. Knopf, 1971.
Arvin, Newton. "Henry James and the Almighty Dollar." *Hound and Horn,* VII (April-June 1934), 434-443.
Barzun, Jacques. "James the Melodramatist." *Kenyon Review,* V (Autumn 1943), 508-521.
Bass, Eben. "Dramatic Scene and *The Awkward Age.*" *PMLA,* LXXIX (March 1964), 148-157.
Beach, Joseph .Warren. *The Method of Henry James* (1918). Revised edition. Philadelphia: Albert Saifer, 1954.
Beebe, Maurice. *Ivory Towers and Sacred Founts: The Artist as Hero in Fiction from Goethe to Joyce.* New York: New York University Press, 1964.
Bell, Millicent. *Edith Wharton and Henry James: The Story of a Friendship.* New York: George Braziller, 1965.
Bersani, Leo. "The Narrator as Center in *The Wings of the Dove.*" *Modern Fiction Studies,* VI (Summer 1960), 131-144.
Bewley, Marius. *The Complex Fate: Hawthorne, Henry James, and Some*

Other American Writers. London: Chatto and Windus, 1952.

—————————. *The Eccentric Design: Form in the Classic American Novel.* New York: Columbia University Press, 1959.

Blackmur, R. P. "In the Country of the Blue." *Kenyon Review,* V (Autumn 1943), 595-617.

Blehl, Vincent S. J. "Freedom and Commitment in James's *Portrait of a Lady.*" *Personalist,* XLII (Summer 1961), 368-381.

Booth, Bradford A. "Henry James and the Economic Motif." *Nineteenth-Century Fiction,* VIII (Sept. 1953), 141-150.

Booth, Wayne C. *The Rhetoric of Fiction.* Chicago: The University of Chicago Press, 1961.

Bowden, Edwin T. *The Themes of Henry James.* New Haven, Connecticut: Yale University Press, 1956.

Broderick, John C. "Nature, Art, and Imagination in *The Spoils of Poynton.*" *Nineteenth-Century Fiction,* XIII (March 1959), 295-312.

Brooks, Van Wyck. *The Pilgrimage of Henry James.* New York: E. P. Dutton and Company, 1925.

Cargill, Oscar. *The Novels of Henry James.* New York: Macmillan, 1961.

Chase, Richard. *The American Novel and Its Tradition.* Garden City, New York: Doubleday Anchor Books, 1957.

Clair, John A. *The Ironic Dimension in the Fiction of Henry James.* Pittsburgh: Duquesne University Press, 1965.

Cooney, Seamus. "Awkward Ages in *The Awkward Age.*" *Modern Language Notes,* LXXV (March 1960), 208-211.

Crews, Frederick C. *The Tragedy of Manners: Moral Drama in the Later Novels of Henry James.* New Haven, Connecticut: Yale University Press, 1957.

Crow, Charles R. "The Style of Henry James: *The Wings of the Dove.*" In Harold C. Martin, ed., *Style in Prose Fiction: English Institute Essays 1958.* New York: Columbia University Press, 1959.

Dubler, Walter. "*The Princess Casamassima:* Its Place in the James Canon." *Modern Fiction Studies,* XII (Spring 1966), 44-60.

Dupee, F. W. *Henry James.* Revised and enlarged edition. Garden City, New York: Doubleday Anchor Books, 1956.

—————————., ed. *The Question of Henry James: A Collection of Critical Essays.* New York: Henry Holt and Company, 1945.

Edel, Leon and Laurence, Dan. *A Bibliography of Henry James.* Second edition, revised. Soho Bibliographies. London: Rupert Hart-Davis, 1961.

Edel, Leon. *Henry James.* Vol. I: *The Untried Years, 1843-1870.* Philadelphia: Lippincott, 1953; Vol. II: *The Conquest of London, 1870-1881.* Philadelphia: Lippincott, 1962; Vol. III: *The Middle Years, 1882-1895.* Philadelphia: Lippincott, 1962; Vol. IV: *The Treacherous Years, 1895-1901.* Philadelphia: Lippincott, 1969; Vol. V: *The Master, 1901-1916.* Philadelphia: Lippincott, 1972.

Edgar, Pelham. *Henry James: Man and Author.* London: Grant Richards Ltd., 1927.

Ferguson, Francis. "James's Idea of Dramatic Form." *Kenyon Review,* V (Autumn 1943), 495-507.

Firebaugh, Joseph. "The Pragmatism of Henry James." *Virginia Quarterly Review,* XXVII (Summer 1951), 419-435.

_____. "The Ververs." *Essays in Criticism,* IV (October 1954), 400-410.

Ford, Ford Madox. *Henry James: A Critical Study.* New York: Dodd, Mead, 1916.

Friend, Joseph H. "The Structure of *The Portrait of a Lady." Nineteenth Century Fiction,* XX (June 1965), 85-95.

Gale, Robert. *The Caught Image: Figurative Language in the Fiction of Henry James.* Chapel Hill, North Carolina: University of North Carolina Press, 1964.

_____. *Plots and Characters in the Fiction of Henry James.* Hamden, Connecticut: Archon Books, 1965.

Gargano, James W. "*The Spoils of Poynton.*" *Sewanee Review,* LXIX (Fall 1961), 650-660.

Geismar, Maxwell. *Henry James and the Jacobites.* New York: Hill and Wang, 1962.

Girling, H. K. " 'Wonder' and 'Beauty' in *The Awkward Age." Essays in Criticism,* VIII (Oct. 1958), 370-380.

Grattan, C. Hartley. *The Three James: A Family of Minds.* New York: New York University Press, 1962.

Greene, Graham. *The Lost Childhood and Other Essays.* London: Heinemann, 1951.

Halliburton, D. G. "Self and Secularization in *The Princess Casamassima." Modern Fiction Studies,* XI (Summer 1965), 116-128.

Hardy, Barbara. *The Appropriate Form: An Essay on the Novel.* London: University of London Athlone Press, 1964.

Harvey, W. J. *Character and the Novel.* Ithaca, New York: Cornell University Press, 1965.

Holland, Laurence Bedwell. *The Expense of Vision: Essays on the Craft of Henry James.* Princeton, New Jersey: Princeton University Press. 1964.

Holland, Norman N. *The Dynamics of Literary Response.* New York: Oxford University Press, 1968.

Hopkins, Viola. "Visual Arts Devices and Parallels in the Fiction of Henry James." *PMLA,* LXXVI (Dec. 1961), 561-574.

Howe, Irving. *Politics and the Novel.* New York: Horizon Press, Inc.. 1957.

Isle, Walter. *Experiments in Form: Henry James's Novels, 1896-1901.* Cambridge, Massachusetts: Harvard University Press, 1968.

James, Henry. *The Ambassadors.* 2 vols. New York: Charles Scribner's Sons, 1909.

_____. *The American.* New York: Charles Scribner's Sons, 1907.

_____. *The American Scene.* New York: Charles Scribner's Sons, 1946.

_____. *The Art of the Novel.* Edited by Richard P. Blackmur. New York: Charles Scribner's Sons, 1934.

_____. *Autobiography: A Small Boy and Others; Notes of a Son and Brother; The Middle Years.* Edited by F. W. Dupee. New York: Criterion Books, Inc., 1956.

_____. *The Awkward Age.* New York: Charles Scribner's Sons, 1908.

_____. *The Bostonians.* London: John Lehmann Ltd., 1952.

——————. *The Complete Plays.* Edited by Leon Edel. Philadelphia: Lippincott, 1949.

——————. *The Complete Tales.* 12 vols. Edited by Leon Edel. London: Rupert Hart-Davis, 1962-1964.

——————. *Daisy Miller.* New York: Charles Scribner's Sons, 1909.

——————. *English Hours.* 2nd ed. Edited by Alma Louise Lowe. London: Heinemann, 1960.

——————. *The Europeans.* London: John Lehmann Ltd., 1952.

——————. *The Golden Bowl.* 2 vols. New York: Charles Scribner's Sons, 1909.

——————. *Hawthorne.* Ithaca, New York: Cornell University Press, 1956.

——————. *Letters.* Selected and edited by Percy Lubbock. 2 vols. London: Macmillan and Co., Limited, 1920.

——————. *Letters to A. C. Benson and Auguste Monod.* Edited by E. F. Benson. London: Elkin Mathews and Marrot, 1930.

——————. *Literary Reviews and Essays on American, English, and French Literature.* Edited by Albert Mordell. New York: Vista House, 1957.

——————. *The Notebooks.* Edited by F. O. Matthiessen and Kenneth B. Murdock. New York: Oxford University Press, 1961.

——————. *The Painter's Eye: Notes and Essays on the Pictorial Arts,* Edited by John L. Sweeney. Cambridge, Massachusetts: Harvard University Press, 1956.

——————. *The Portrait of a Lady.* 2 vols. New York: Charles Scribner's Sons, 1908.

——————. *The Princess Casamassima.* 2 vols. New York: Charles Scribner's Sons, 1908.

——————. *Roderick Hudson.* New York: Charles Scribner's Sons, 1907.

——————. *The Sacred Fount.* London: Rupert Hart-Davis, 1959.

——————. *The Scenic Art: Notes on Acting and the Drama, 1872-1901.* Edited by Allan Wade. London: Rupert Hart-Davis, 1949.

——————. *Selected Letters.* Edited by Leon Edel. Garden City, New York: Doubleday Anchor Books, 1960.

——————. *Selected Literary Criticism.* Edited by Morris Shapira. London: Heinemann, 1963.

——————. *The Spoils of Poynton.* New York: Charles Scribner's Sons, 1908.

——————. *The Tragic Muse.* 2 vols. New York: Charles Scribner's Sons, 1908.

——————. *Washington Square.* London: Macmillan and Co., 1883.

——————. *What Maisie Knew.* New York: Charles Scribner's Sons, 1908.

——————. *The Wings of the Dove.* 2 vols. New York: Charles Scribner's Sons, 1909.

Jefferson, D. W. *Henry James and the Modern Reader.* Edinburgh: Oliver and Boyd, 1960.

Kelley, Cornelia Pulsifer. *The Early Development of Henry James.* Rev. ed. Urbana, Illinois: University of Illinois Press, 1965.

Kettle, Arnold. *An Introduction to the English Novel.* 2 vols. New York: Harper and Brothers, 1960.

Koch, Stephen. "Transcendence in *The Wings of the Dove.*" *Modern Fiction Studies,* XII (Spring 1966), 93-102.

Krause, Sidney J. "James's Revisions of the Style of *The Portrait of a Lady.*" *American Literature,* XXX (March 1958), 67-88.

Krook, Dorothea. *The Ordeal of Consciousness in Henry James.* Cambridge: Cambridge University Press, 1962.

Leavis, F. R. *The Great Tradition: George Eliot, Henry James, Joseph Conrad.* New York: George Stewart, 1949.

Lebowitz, Naomi. *The Imagination of Loving: Henry James's Legacy to the Novel.* Detroit, Michigan: Wayne State University Press, 1965.

Levin, Gerald. "Why Does Vanderbank Not Propose?" *University of Kansas City Review,* XXVII (June 1961), 314-318.

Levy, Leo B. *Versions of Melodrama: A Study of the Fiction and Drama of Henry James, 1865-1897.* Berkeley: University of California Press, 1957.

Luecke, Sister Jane Marie. "*The Princess Casamassima:* Hyacinth's Fallible Consciousness." *Modern Philology,* LX (May 1963), 274-280.

Mackenzie, Manfred. "Ironic Melodrama in *The Portrait of a Lady.*" *Modern Fiction Studies,* XII (Spring 1966), 7-23.

Matthiessen, F. O. *Henry James: The Major Phase.* New York: Oxford University Press, 1944.

McLean, Robert C. "The Subjective Adventures of Fleda Vetch." *American Literature,* XXXVI (March 1964), 12-30.

Nowell-Smith, Simon. *The Legend of the Master.* London: Constable, 1947.

O'Grady, Walter. "On Plot in Modern Fiction: Hardy, James, and Conrad." *Modern Fiction Studies,* XI (Summer 1965), 107-115.

Oliver, Clinton. "Henry James as a Social Critic." *Antioch Review,* VII (June 1947), 243-258.

Poirier, Richard. *The Comic Sense of Henry James: A Study of the Early Novels.* London: Chatto and Windus, 1960.

Putt, S. Gorley. *Henry James: A Reader's Guide.* Ithaca, New York: Cornell University Press, 1966.

Quinn, Patrick. "Morals and Motives in *The Spoils of Poynton.*" *Sewanee Review,* LXII (Autumn 1954), 563-577.

Reilly, Robert J. "Henry James and the Morality of Fiction." *American Literature,* XXXIX (March 1967), 1-30.

Roberts, Morris. *Henry James's Criticism.* Cambridge, Massachusetts: Harvard University Press, 1929.

Roper, Alan H. "The Moral and Metaphorical Meaning of *The Spoils of Poynton.*" *American Literature,* XXXII (May 1960), 182-196.

Rosenzweig, Saul. "The Ghost of Henry James: A Study in Thematic Apperception." *Partisan Review,* XI (Fall 1944), 435-455.

Sandeen, Ernest. "*The Wings of the Dove* and *The Portrait of a Lady:* A Study of Henry James's Later Phase." *PMLA,* LXIX (Dec. 1954), 1060-1075.

Sharp, Sister M. Corona. *The "Confidante" in Henry James: Evolution and Moral Value of a Fictive Character.* Notre Dame, Indiana: University of Notre Dame Press, 1963.

Snow, Lotus. "The Disconcerting Poetry of Mary Temple: A Comparison of the Imagery of *The Portrait of a Lady* and *The Wings of the Dove.*" *New England Quarterly,* XXXI (Sept. 1958), 312-339.

Spender, Stephen. *The Destructive Element: A Study of Modern Writers and Beliefs.* London: J. Cape, 1935.

Stallman, Robert Wooster. *The Houses that James Built, and Other Literary*

Studies. East Lansing, Michigan: Michigan State University Press, 1961.
——————. " 'The Sacred Rage': The Time-Theme in *The Ambassadors.*"
        Modern Fiction Studies, III (Spring 1957), 41-56.
Stafford, William T. "Emerson and the James Family." *American Literature,*
        XXIV (Jan. 1953), 433-461.
Stevenson, Elizabeth. *The Crooked Corridor: A Study of Henry James.* New
        York: Macmillan, 1949.
Stone, Edward. *The Battle and the Books: Some Aspects of Henry James.*
        Athens, Ohio: Ohio University Press, 1964.
Tanner, Tony. "The Fearful Self: Henry James's *The Portrait of a Lady.*" *Crit-
        ical Quarterly,* VII (Autumn 1965), 205-219.
——————. *The Reign of Wonder: Naivety and Reality in American Liter
        ature.* New York: Cambridge University Press, 1965.
Tilley, Wesley H. *The Background of The Princess Casamassima.* Gainesville
        Florida: University of Florida Monographs, 1961.
Trilling, Lionel. *"The Princess Casamassima,"* in *The Liberal Imagination: Es
        says on Literature and Society.* New York: The Viking Press, 1950.
Vivas, Eliseo. "William and Henry (Two Notes)." *Kenyon Review,* V (Autum
        1943), 580-594.
Volpe, Edmund L. "James's Theory of Sex in Fiction." *Nineteenth-Centur
        Fiction,* XIII (Spring 1958), 36-47.
——————. "The Spoils of Art." *Modern Language Notes,* LXXIV (Nc
        1959), 601-607.
Ward, J. A. *The Imagination of Disaster: Evil in the Fiction of Henry Jam
        Lincoln, Nebraska: University of Nebraska Press, 1961.
——————. *The Search for Form: Studies in the Structure of James's F
        tion,* Chapel Hill, North Carolina: The University of North Carolina
        Press, 1967.
Warren, Austin. *Rage for Order: Essays in Criticism.* Chicago: University of
        Chicago Press, 1948.
Wasiolek, Edward. "Maisie: Pure or Corrupt?" *College English,* XXII (D
        1960), 167-172.
Wasserstrom, William. *Heiress of All the Ages: Sex and Sentiment in the Gen
        teel Tradition.* Minneapolis: University of Minnesota Press, 1959.
Wegelin, Christof. *The Image of Europe in Henry James.* Dallas: Southern
        Methodist University Press, 1958.
West, Rebecca. *Henry James.* London: Nisbet & Co. Ltd., 1916.
Wharton, Edith. *A Backward Glance.* New York: D. Appleton-Century Com-
        pany Inc., 1934.
Wiesenfarth, Joseph. *Henry James and the Dramatic Analogy.* New York:
        Fordham University Press, 1963.
Wilson, Edmund. *The Triple Thinkers.* Revised edition. New York: Oxford
        University Press, 1948.
Winters, Yvor. *In Defense of Reason.* Denver: Alan Swallow, 1947
Woodcock, George. "Henry James and the Conspirators." *Sewanee Review,*
        LX (Spring 1952), 219-229.
Wright, Walter F. *The Madness of Art: A Study of Henry James.* Lincoln,
        Nebraska: University of Nebraska Press, 1962.